American Indian Poetry:

An Anthology of Songs and Chants

American Indian Poetry:

An Anthology of Songs and Chants

EDITED BY

GEORGE W. CRONYN

With an Introduction by
MARY AUSTIN

Illustrated by
J. B. PLATT

LIVERIGHT

NEW YORK

*This anthology was originally published under
the title THE PATH ON THE RAINBOW:
An Anthology of Songs and Chants From The
Indians of North America.*

2.987654321
SBN: 87140-044-8
Library of Congress Catalog Card Number: 73-133483
Manufactured in the United States of America.

DEDICATION

To those who have labored faithfully in the collection and transcription of the Art Forms of a Vanishing Race this book is respectfully dedicated.

Many of the songs and chants herein translated are very ancient; a number are modern, but none exhibit the slightest traces of European influence; they are genuine American Classics.

ACKNOWLEDGMENTS

To *Poetry, a Magazine of Verse,* for permission to reprint "Early Moon," by Carl Sandburg; "Along the South Star Trail," "Sa-a Narai," and "On the Warpath," by Dr. Frank S. Gordon; "Listening," "Buffalo Dance," "Where the Fight Was," "The Wind," "Courtship," and "Parting," by Alice Corbin; "Neither Spirit nor Bird," and "Prayer to the Mountain Spirit," by Mary Austin; "Summer Dawn," "Song of the Search," "Song of the Whip-Plaiting," "Song of the Young Mother," "Change-Song," "Spring to the Earth-Witch," and "Chief Capilano Greets His Namesake at Dawn," by Constance Lindsay Skinner.

To the following magazines for permission to reprint interpretations by Constance Lindsay Skinner: *Scribner's Magazine,* "Wild Woman's Lullaby"; *Sunset Magazine,* "Lover's Hymn"; *The Delineator,* "Autumn Dawn"; *Others Magazine,* "Song of Basket Weaving." Miss Skinner also contributed "The Bilqula Death Song" and "Three Songs from the Haida." For additional work by Mary Austin, permission to reprint was granted by *McClure's Magazine,* "Song of the Hills"; *The Forum Magazine,* "Indian Songs"; *Everybody's,* "Medicine Songs."

The "Songs of the Yuma," by J. P. Harrington; the Chinook, Eskimo, Kwakiutl Songs by Franz Boas; the Navajo Gambling Songs and "The Songs in the Garden of the House of God," by Washington Matthews, are reprinted by permission from the *Journal of American Folk Lore.* "Micmac War Songs" by S. T. Rand, and "Ojibwa Songs" by H. H. Schoolcraft and Charles Fenno Hoffman are reprinted from these authors' published volumes. The "Abanaki Songs" by John Reade appeared in the *Transactions of the Royal Society of Canada.* "The Lost Lagoon," and "The Song My Paddle Sings," by Pauline Johnson, are reprinted by permission of the Musson Book Co., Toronto. Permission was obtained from Little, Brown & Co. to reprint "Four Spirit Songs from California," translated by Jeremiah Curtin.

"The Haida Songs" by J. R. Swanton are from publications of the American Ethnological Society. Space does not permit the publishers to present "The Hako: A Pawnee Ceremony," by Alice Fletcher, in full. It will be found in its complete form in the Twenty-Second Annual Report, Bureau of Ethnology, Smithsonian Institution. The translations by Natalie Curtis are reprinted by permission of Harper & Bros. from *The Indians' Book*, recommended to the reader for its intensive study of Indian songs and their sources.

From *Poetry, a Magazine of Verse*, came the inspiration for this anthology; the editor is grateful, also, to its generous contributors for many interpretations. Unless otherwise specified, all translations are from bulletins or reports of the Bureau of Ethnology, Smithsonian Institution, members of whose staff were most helpful . . . The designs in this book were adapted by Mr. J. B. Platt from authentic Indian motifs, and have been arranged according to the cultural divisions of the poems so that the two art forms will be found side by side.

CONTENTS

CONTENTS

CONTENTS

SONGS FROM THE NORTHWEST COAST

SONGS FROM THE FAR NORTH

INTERPRETATIONS

Constance Lindsay Skinner

Mary Austin

CONTENTS

(Interpretations)

INTRODUCTION

The poetic faculty is, of all man's modes,
the most responsive to natural environ-
ment, the most sensitive and the truest rec-
ord of his reactions to its skyey influences,
its floods, forests, morning colors. It is
the first to register the rise of his spirits
to the stimulus of new national ideals. If
this were not so there would be no such
thing as nationality in art, and it is only by
establishing some continuity with the ear-
liest instances of such reaction that we can
be at all sure that American poetic genius
has struck its native note. Therefore it be-
comes appropriate and important that this
collection of American Indian verse should
be brought to public notice at a time when
the whole instinctive movement of the
American people is for a deeper footing
in their native soil. It is the certificate of
our adoption, that the young genius of our
time should strike all unconsciously on this
ancient track to the High Places.

Poetic art in America at the time it be-
gan to be overlaid by European culture,

had reached a mark close to that of the Greeks at the beginning of the Homeric era. The lyric was well developed, the epic was nascent, and the drama was still in the Satyris stage of development, a rude dance ritual about an altar or a sacrificial fire. Neither poetry nor drama were yet divorced from singing, and all art was but half-born out of the Great Mystery. Magic was sung, and songs had magic power. Both were accompanied by appropriate bodily movement, so that an Indian will say indifferently, I cannot sing that dance, or I cannot dance that song. Words, melody and movement were as much mixed as the water of a river with its own ripples and its rate of flowing. Hum a few bars of a plainsman's familiar song, and he will say, puzzled, "It ought to be a war song," but without the words he will scarcely identify it. Words may become obsolete so that the song is untranslatable, but so long as enough of it remains to hold together the primary emotional impulse out of which it sprang, the Indian finds it worthy to be sung. He is, indeed, of the opinion that "White man's songs, they talk too much."

This partly explains why most Indian songs are songs for occasions. The rest of the explanation lies in the fact that songs

have magic power. Tirawa, Wokonda, The
Friend of the Soul of Man, is in every-
thing; in the field we plant, the stone we
grind with, the bear we kill. By singing,
the soul of the singer is put in harmony
with the essential Essence of Things.
There are songs for every possible adven-
ture of tribal life; songs for setting out on
a journey, a song for the first sight of your
destination, and a song to be sung by your
wife for your safe return. Many of these
songs occur detached from everything but
the occasion from which they sprang, such
as the women's grinding song, measured
to the *plump, plump!* of the mealing stone,
or the Paddle Song which follows the swift
rhythm of the stroke. Others, less descrip-
tive and retaining always something of a
sacred character, occur originally as num-
bers in the song sequences by which are
celebrated the tribal Mysteries.

Back of every Indian ceremony lies a
story, the high moments of which are
caught up in song, while the burden of the
narrative is carried by symbolic rite and
dance. The unequal social development of
contemporaneous tribes affords examples
from every phase of structural develop-
ment from the elemental dance punctuated
by singing exclamations to the Mountain
Chant of the Zuni in which the weight of

the story has broken down the verse vari-
ants into strong simple forms capable of
being carried in a single memory. Half-
way between them is the ritual sequence of
the Midéwan.

The practical necessity of being pre-
served and handed on by word of mouth
only, must be constantly borne in mind in
considering the development of Indian
verse forms.

It operated to keep the poetry tied to
its twin-born melody, which assisted mem-
ory, and was constantly at work modifying
the native tendency to adjust the rhythm to
every changing movement of the story.
Ancient Chippeway singers kept ideo-
graphic birch bark memoranda of their
songs, and wampum belts commemorated
the events that gave use to them, but the
songs themselves came down from their
ancient sources hundreds of years in the
stream of human memory shaped by its
limitations.

From the Zuni Creation Cycle with its
sustained narrative style to the Homeric
Epic is but one poetic bound, the space be-
tween them, represented in old world liter-
ature by the Norse Sagas and the Kale-
vala, indicated but not filled, in America,
by prose relations. It is probable that if
we had anything like adequate records of

the literature of vanished tribes, this pre-Homeric period would show notable examples of epic stuff. Nobody really knows how the Walam Olum or the Creek Migration Myths were recited. They embodied whole epochs of tribal history, to which the known literary remains were merely the nemonic key, a tally of significant items. In every tribe are floating songs which appear to be fragments from a story sequence the key of which has been lost, and it is not unlikely that records like the Red Score would have owned complete, if detached, narratives of the historic events so slightly indicated, some of which may yet yield themselves to the patient researcher.

For the casual reader more interest attaches to the personal songs, the lullabys, love songs, most of all the man's *own* song which he makes of his great moment. This is a peculiar personal possession. No one may sing it without his permission. He may bestow it on a friend, or bequeath it to the tribe on his death, but it is also possible that he may die without having sung it to anyone but his god.

On one occasion in the high Sierras I observed my Indian packer going apart at a certain hour each day to shuffle rhythmically with his feet and croon to himself.

To my inquiry he said it was a song which he had made, to be sung by himself and his wife when they were apart from one another.

It had no words; it was just a song. Wherever they were they turned each in the direction he supposed the other to be, when the sun was a bow-shot above the edge of the heavens, and sang together. This is the sort of incident which gives the true value of song in aboriginal life. It is not the words which are potent, but the states of mind evoked by singing, states which the simple savage conceived as being supernally good for him. He evoked them therefore on all his most personal occasions. Poetry is the Path on the Rainbow by which the soul climbs; it lays hold on the Friend of the Soul of Man. Such exalted states are held to be protective and curative. Medicine men sing for their patients, and, in times of war, wives gather around the Chief's woman and sing for the success of their warriors.

"Calling on Zeus by the names of Victory" as Euripides puts it.

It is this inherent power of poetry to raise the psychic plane above the accidents of being, which gives meaning to the custom of the Death Song. As he sees his moment approaching, the Indian throws

himself, by some profound instinct of self-
preservation, into the highest frame of
mind attainable. When men in battle
broke into the death song, they had com-
mitted themselves to the last desperate ad-
venture. Dying of enfeebling sickness,
their friends came and sang around them.
One such I heard, the death song of a
Yokut Song Maker. It was very simple:

> "All my life
> I have been seeking,
> Seeking!

What more than this have the schools
taught us!

Of Indian meters there has been no com-
petent study made. The whole problem of
form is inextricably complicated with
melody and movement. The necessity of
making his verse conform to a dance, prob-
ably accounts for the liberal use of mean-
ingless syllables. To our ear no specific
forms seem indicated, yet that the Indians
recognize a certain correspondence between
form and meaning is certain. They will
readily classify songs of other tribes in
unknown tongues into songs of love or war
or magic. The genius of the tribal lan-
guage is a determining factor. No clum-
siness of translation can quite disguise the

—from our point of view—superior sing-
ableness of Chippeway verse. In general,
poetry of forest dwellers is more lyric than
the songs of mountain and mesa. An in-
quiry which I once made into the psychol-
ogy of the Indian sign language with a view
to discovering a possible relation between
it and Greek manual gesture as displayed
in ancient graphic art, led to the conclusion
that Indian rhythms arise rather in the
centre of self-preservation than of self-con-
sciousness. Which is only another way of
saying that poetry is valued primarily by
the aboriginal for the reaction it produces
within himself rather than for any effect
he is able to produce on others by means
of it. This is true even of that class of
songs which originates wholly in the desire
to affect the fortunes or well being of oth-
ers, songs of healing and magic formulae.

The first stage of Indian magic is the
rise of the singer on his own song to a
plane of power; only while he is in this
plane is he able to bring the wish of his
client to pass. It is a natural process of
deterioration which leads to the song being
thought of as having potency in itself.

Magic songs can generally be recog-
nized by the form of affirmation in which
they are cast, as in the Winnebago Love

Song, which is not really a song of love, but a song to secure success in love,

> Whosoe'r I look upon
> He becomes love crazed.

or the Cherokee formula to insure the constancy of the beloved, and the Micmac vengeance song

> Death I make,
> Singing.

Among the Navajo the magic effect is made certain by the four-fold repetition of the affirming phrase, four being a sacred number.

These are all items which have to be taken into account in interpreting American Indian poetry. It is in the very nature of primitive verse that it should require interpretation, even among the audiences for whom it is originally intended. For verse is to the Red singer but a shorthand note to his emotions, a sentence or two, a phrase out of the heart of the situation. It is the "inside song" alone which is important. Says the Medicine Man, explaining these matters, "You see Injun man singin' an' cryin' while he sing. It ain't what he singin' make him cry; iss what the song make him think, thass what he cryin' about."

This inside song may be a fleeting instant of revelation, or a very long story . . . as if one should try in the Zuni fashion to compress the whole Christian myth into one bitter cry,

> My God! My God!
> Why hast Thou deserted me?

> Hi-ihiya, naiho-o,
>   It is finished,
>   In beauty it is finished
>   Nai-ho-o!

Whole cycles of tribal or personal experience can lie behind some such simple but absolute phrasing. It is this hidden beauty for which the interpreter must dig deep into aboriginal life.

The Ghost Dance songs included in this collection are scarcely intelligible until the reader realizes that they are supposed to be the flashes of revelation brought from the dead in dreams, foretelling the approach of a spiritual revival.

Thus it came to the Cheyenne:

> I bring the whirlwind

That you may know one another

We shall live again!

To the Piaute also

> Fog, fog,
> Lightning, lightning,
> Whirlwind, whirlwind.

and then

> The cottonwoods are growing tall
> They are growing tall and green.

For to the Piaute from his flat Reservation on Walker River, the faint young green of the cottonwoods is the first sign of that new growth which follows after seasonal storms. Any adequate rendering of these songs would have to convey in native figures all this sense of immanent world-overturning and spiritual reëstablishment in the Oneness of God and the Brotherhood of man.

(It is I who wear the Morning Star on my
        forehead . . .
All that grows upon the earth is mine
Says the Father.)

Thus interpreted they would rank with

the prophetic utterances of the herdsman
of Tekoa. It is quite possible, indeed, that
in time all these ghostly songs would have
been detached from their obscure authors
and ascribed to the Messiah of the Ghost
Dance, who would have been reckoned
among the major prophets.

For such illuminating gleams that Indian
poetry can throw on the genesis of inspired
literature, its study would be worth while,
even if without the renewal of our native
stock of poetic forms and figures.

It is probable that the best Indian poetry
has been lost to us in the stamping out of
superior tribes.

This would be particularly the case in the
south, where social development had
reached a stage which only the pueblos and
the Five Nations of western New York ap-
proached.

Miss Convers has shown us in the frag-
ments of Iroquois ritual something of what
might still be recovered from the remnants
of that race, but this single example from
the forgotten tribe of Tenasa, on the shore
of the Missi-sippu seems to me to overleap
all time and space and touch the hidden
source of Greek inspiration. It is a mar-
riage song, the faithful translation of an
unliterary explorer, Greek in its mode, and

in a certain tender irony of mood, but with
touches to which only a full knowledge of
Indian thought can give their full value,
for all of which I venture to give it the iso-
lation of its native quality.

Tiakens, thou buildest a house,
Thou bringest a wife to live in it.

Thou art married, Tiakens, thou art mar-
        ried,
Thou wilt become famous, thy children wilt
        name thee among the elders.
Think of Tiakens as an old man!

By what name is thy bride known,
Is she beautiful?
Are her eyes soft as the light of the moon?
Is she a strong woman?
Didst thou understand her signs as she
        danced to thee?
I know not whether thou lovest her,
        Tiakens,
What saidst the old man, her father, when
        you asked for his pretty daughter?
What betrothal gifts didst thou give her?

Rejoice, Tiakens, be glad, be happy,
Build thyself a happy home.
This is the song of its building.

The single line which identifies the song of Tiakens as intrinsically American is that one which inquires:

Didst thou understand her signs when she danced to thee? embodying as it does a very widespread aboriginal belief that in the dance and song, more than in any other medium, a maiden revealed the physical capacity and the power of sustained emotion which fitted her for marriage. Since when, and with what unhappy results, have *we* forgotten that creative emotion is a qualification for marriage! We do shallowly indeed when we dismiss the dance and song as mere millinery of courtship. They are the speech of the spirit identifying itself with cosmic forces. I do not know whether or not the Tenasa had the custom known on the Pacific Coast as the Dance of Marriageable Maidens, but I know that if you cut deeply into any Indian poem it yields that profound and palpitant humanism without which no literary art can endure.

Failure to realize the living background of Indian art has led to singular misinterpretation, in a class of songs common to every tribe, and almost invariably translated as love songs by the novice. These are the songs of the Mystics, Songs of Seeking. They record the unavailing

search of the soul for the Absolute, for
touch of that Great Mystery which is the
object of the Indian's profoundest aspira-
tion. Two such songs may be found in
Frederick Burton's collection of Ojibway
music, done into rather sentimental love
ditties, the "Lake's Sheen" and the "Birch
Bark Canoe," though their character as re-
ligious songs was so plainly marked that
Mr. Burton himself commented on the sin-
gularity of Indian sweethearts forever get-
ting themselves lost and requiring to be
sought. It is well to remember before
attempting the interpretation of an Indian
love song, that the great Mystics have al-
ways appropriated the intimate language
of the heart for the soul's quest. As will
be seen from the examples which Mr.
Cronyn has included in his collection, the
work of interpreting our treasure of
Indian verse has been but lightly begun.
While some of these, notably Miss Corbin's
"Across the River" leave nothing to be
desired of the spirit, form and content of
the original, many others have had frankly
to sacrifice one of them.

In my own interpretations I have been
feeling rather for a full expression of In-
dian thought, than for lyric quality.

And in any case, mine is not a singing

gift. All Indian verse is either sung or chanted, but the difficulty of fitting Indian rhythms to European music is only surpassed by the difficulty of getting Indian music arranged in European notation.

The long divided Muses of poetry, music and dance must come together again for the absolute rendering. Enough cannot be said in praise of the work of Miss Fletcher, Natalie Curtis, Frank Cushing and Washington Mathews, to mention no others, for the clarity and sincerity of their literal translations. The interpreter's work is all before him. I know of no task so salutory to the poet who would, first of all, put himself in touch with the resident genius of his own land.

MARY AUSTIN.

American Indian Poetry:

An Anthology of Songs and Chants

SONGS FROM THE
EASTERN WOODLANDS

EARLY MOON

The baby moon, a canoe, a silver papoose
canoe, sails and sails in the Indian
West.

A ring of silver foxes, a mist of silver
foxes, sit and sit around the Indian
moon.

One yellow star for a runner, and rows of
blue stars for more runners, keep a
line of watchers.

O foxes, baby moon, runners, you are the
panel of memory, fire-white writing
tonight of the Red Man's dreams.

Who squats, legs crossed, and arms folded,
matching its look against the moon-
face, the star-faces, of the West?

Who are the Mississippi Valley ghosts, of
copper foreheads, riding wiry ponies
in the night?—no bridles, love arms on
the pony necks, riding in the night, a
long old trail?

Why do they always come back when the
silver foxes sit around the early moon,
a silver papoose, in the Indian West?

THE PARTED LOVERS

(*Abanaki*)

I

THE MAN SINGS

My parents think they can separate me
    from the girl I love;
We have vowed to love each other while
    we live.
Their commands are vain: we shall see
    each other while the world lasts.
 Yes! let them say or do what they like;
    we shall see each other while the rocks
    stand.

THE WOMAN SINGS

Here I sit on this point, whence I can see
    the man that I love.
Our people think that they can sever us;
    but I shall see him while the world
    lasts.
Here shall I remain, in sight of the one
    I love.

II

THE GIRL DESERTED BY HER JEALOUS COMPANIONS SINGS

Now I am left on this lonely island to die—
No one to hear the sound of my voice.
Who will bury me when I die?
Who will sing my death-song?
My false friends leave me here to die
    alone;
Like a wild beast, I am left on this island
    to die.
I wish the wind spirit would carry my cry
    to my love!
My love is swift as the deer; he would
    speed through the forest to find me.
Now I am left on this lonely island to die.
I wish the wind spirit would carry my cry
    to my love!
My love is as swift as the deer; he would
    speed through the forest to find me;
Now I am left on this lonely island to die.
I wish the spirit of air would carry my
    breath to my love.
My love's canoe, like sunlight, would shoot
    through the water to my side;
But I am left on this lonely island to die,
    with no one to pity me but the little
    birds.

My love is brave and strong; but, when he
hears my fate, his heart will break.
And I am on this lonely island to die.
Now the night comes on, and all is silent
but the owl.
He sings a mournful song to his mate, in
pity for me.
I will try to sleep.
I wish the night spirit to hear my song; he
will tell my love of my fate; and when
I awake, I shall see the one I love.
I am on this lonely island to die.

III

HER LOVER SEES HER IN A DREAM AND, GOING
TO SEARCH FOR HER, SINGS

Come, my beloved, let us go up that shining
mountain, and sit together on that
shining mountain; there we will watch
the Sun go down in beauty from that
shining place.
There we will sit, till the Night Traveler
arises in beauty about the shining
mountain; we will watch him as he
climbs to the beautiful skies.
We will also watch the little Stars follow-
ing their chief.
We will also watch the Northern Lights
playing their game of ball in their
cold, glistening country.

There we will sit, on the beautiful mountain, and listen to the Thunder beating his drum.

We will see the flashes from the lit pipe of the Lightning.

We will see the great Whirlwind race with Squall.

There we· will sit, until all creatures drowse.

There we will hear the great Owl sing his usual song: "Go-to-sleep-all," and see all animals obey his call.

There we will sit in beauty on the mountain, and watch the small Stars in their sleepless flight.

They do not mind the song, "go-to-sleep-all"; neither will we mind it, but sit more closely together, and think of nothing but ourselves, on the beautiful mountain.

Again, the "go-to-sleep all" will be heard, and the Night Traveler will come closer to warn us that all are sleeping, except ourselves and the little Stars.

They and their chief are coursing along, and our minds go with them.

Then the Owl sleeps; no more is heard "go - to - sleep - all"; the Lightnings flash afar; the great pipe is going out;

the Thunder ceases beating his drum;
and though our bodies urge us to be
sleeping, we sit in beauty still upon
the shining mountain.

VENGEANCE SONG
(*Micmac*)

Death I make, singing
Heh-yeh! heh-yeh! heh-yeh! heh-yeh!
Bones I hack, singing
Heh-yeh! heh-yeh! heh-yeh! heh-yeh!
Death I make, singing
Heh-yeh! heh-yeh! heh-yeh! heh!

IROQUOIS RITUAL OF FIRE AND DARKNESS

*The members of the Ho-no-tci-no-ga Society
assemble. Now the Medicine Doctor or Shaman
casts the sacred tobacco on the medicine-blaze,
and in a low voice he chants:*

Great Spirit who puts us to sleep in dark-
ness,
We thank thee for the silences of darkness.
(Singer)
Now I ask blessing and make prayers.
*(He sprinkles sacred tobacco on the fire. Then
he speaks to the Invisible :)*
Now I give you tobacco,
You, the great Darkness!

(To the Thunder Spirit)

Now we act as we offer you tobacco!
You love it most of all offerings.
With it you will hear us better
And not tire of our talking
But love us with all power
Beyond all treasures
Or spreading of words through the air!
All men traveling under great heaven
You have invited, your grandchildren and
    all nations;
Oh you, maker of noise,
You, the great Thunderer!
Your grandchildren wish to thank you!
All your grandchildren have asked me
To offer this tobacco upon the mountain
    to you!

(Speaking to the Great Spirit)

You the All-maker,
Above-all-high
Best Friend of people!
We ask you to help us!
We implore your favor!
I have spoken.

   The lights are extinguished, leaving the assembly in total darkness. The Watcher of the Medicine uncovers the bundles, exposing it to the air, and as he does so a faint luminous cloud hovers over the table and disappears. Now the Chanter gives the signal and the members sing:

THE CHANT OF DARKNESS

Wait here in the darkness!
Come, all you who listen,
Go the magic journey:
Now the sky is empty
Of all sun-and-star-shine;
Come, we lose our footing.
Night no friend of ours is;
She has shut her eyelids.
Moon who has forgotten
Lets us wait in darkness!

*Now the chiefs take their rattles, shaking them
softly as the Chanter sings and members of the
clan give the whip-poor-will cry.*

THE CHANT OF INVITATION TO THE WHIP-POOR-WILL TOTEM
(*Chorus*)

Thus sings the Whip-poor-will,
Follow me, follow me!
Thus speaks the Chief to him,
Yes, I will follow you!
Lo! the night darkening
Stalks through the shadow-land;
No light to beckon us
Murmurs the waterfall,
Thus sings the river-voice!
Someone is nearing us,
Creeping upon us close,
Two fires of eyes are close

Lighting the forest path—
Hear how his breath blows by!
Fol-low me, fol-low me,—
So sings the whip-poor-will!
Yes, I am following—
Thus the Chief answers him.

Cries announce that the Wolf and his mate have entered the room.

Hark the trees whispering
Bend their old bodies low,
Not the strong North Wind's hand
Nay, but One great and swift
Parts them with whistling breath!
Hark! how the thickets snap!
Fearless the footfalls pass
Pushing the trees apart
Great horns dividing them.

(Again the Whip-poor-will chorus)

Now Buck and Doe, with cries, enter. The song continues:

How I go shivering!
No snow is falling now,
Where hides the sun his fire?
Something swift-footed comes
Roaring and warning me!
Eyes of the night it blinds,
Falling like heavy mist!
Now it creeps close to me,
Warning and beckoning
Where the black forest looms.

(*Whip-poor-will chorus*)
*The Bear and his mate have come and the song
goes on:*

How the wind whistles now!
No one dares race with it.
Great trees bend low to it,
Rivers fight back to it,
Roaring and splashing it!
Hear how its strong wings beat
Deep in the gusty sky!
High through the night it flies
Whistling and screaming, still
Hunting the prey that runs!

(*Whip-poor-will chorus*)
*The Hawk and its mate are announced. Then
rites symbolizing the dangers of the forest tangles
and swampy horrors are performed. According
to the legend Eagle must dismiss the meeting.
His coming, which is imitated on the small flute,
announces the day. As the dawn-light penetrates
the ceremonial place the last chorus is chanted of*

THE EAGLE

Deep the dew-water falls
No one comes close to me!
Where are you, Whip-poor-will?
Why am I waiting now
Calling you, calling you?
Screaming the night away
With his great feathers spread

Catching the darkness up
I hear the Eagle-bird
Pulling the blanket back
From the east, sleeping still.
How swift he flies, bearing the sun to the
    morning;
See how he perches there on the trail of
    of the east-sky.
Whip-poor-will, Whip-poor-will,
No more I follow thee!
When night springs up again
Will you cry, "Follow me?"

*The singing ends and the matrons bring in food
and distribute it to all.*

FIRE-FLY SONG
(Ojibwa)

Flitting white-fire insects!
Wandering small-fire beasts!
Wave little stars about my bed!
Weave little stars into my sleep!
Come, little dancing white-fire bug,
Come, little flitting white-fire beast!
Light me with your white-flame magic,
Your little star-torch.

CALLING-ONE'S-OWN
(Ojibwa)

Awake! flower of the forest, sky-treading
    bird of the prairie.

Awake! awake! wonderful fawn-eyed One.
When you look upon me I am satisfied; as
    flowers that drink dew.
The breath of your mouth is the fragrance
    of flowers in the morning,
Your breath is their fragrance at evening
    in the moon-of-fading-leaf.
Do not the red streams of my veins run
    toward you
As forest-streams to the sun in the moon
    of bright nights?
When you are beside me my heart sings; a
    branch it is, dancing,
Dancing before the Wind-spirit in the
    moon of strawberries.
When you frown upon me, beloved, my
    heart grows dark—
A shining river the shadows of clouds
    darken,
Then with your smiles comes the sun and
    makes to look like gold
Furrows the cold wind drew in the water's
    face.
Myself! behold me! blood of my beating
    heart.
Earth smiles—the waters smile—even the
    sky-of-clouds smiles—but I,
I lose the way of smiling when you are not
    near,
Awake! awake! my beloved.

OJIBWA WAR SONGS

I

Hear my voice, Birds of War!
I prepare a feast for you to feed on;
I see you cross the enemy's lines;
Like you I shall go.
I wish the swiftness of your wings;
I wish the vengeance of your claws;
I muster my friends;
I follow your flight.
Ho, you young men warriors,
Bear your angers to the place of fighting!

II

From the south they came, Birds of War—
Hark! to their passing scream.
I wish the body of the fiercest,
As swift, as cruel, as strong.
I cast my body to the chance of fighting.
Happy I shall be to lie in that place,
In that place where the fight was,
Beyond the enemy's line.

III

Here on my breast have I bled!
See—see! these are fighting-scars!
Mountains tremble at my yell!
I strike for life.

LOVE-SONG
(*Winnebago*)

Whomsoe'er look I upon
    He becomes love-crazed;
Whomsoe'er speak I unto,
    He becomes love-crazed;
Whomsoe'er whisper I to,
    He becomes love-crazed;
All men who love women,
Them I rule, them I rule,
        My friend;
Whom I touch, whom I touch,
    He becomes love-crazed.

HOLY SONG
(*Winnebago*)

(Saith the Spirit,
"Dream, oh, dream again,
And tell of me,
    Dream thou!")

Into solitude went I
And wisdom was revealed to me.
    (Saith the Spirit,
    "Dream, oh, dream again,
    And tell of me,
        Dream thou!")

Let the whole world hear me,
Wise am I!

(Now saith the Spirit,
"Tell of me,
    Dream thou!")

All was revealed to me;
From the beginning
Know I all, hear me!
All was revealed to me!
    (Now saith the Spirit,
    "Tell of me,
        Dream thou!")

SACRED MIDÉ SONGS
(*Ojibwa*)
Drifting snow,
    why do I sing?

The Sun and Moon,
Their bodies
    shine over the world
    unto me as unto you, my Midé
    friend.

SONGS OF THE CHIPPEWA
HEALING SONG

They are in close consultation
    with their heads together
    Wenabojo
    and his grandmother.

LOVE-CHARM

What are you saying to me?
I am arrayed like the roses
    and beautiful as they.

I AM WALKING

Toward calm and shady places
    I am walking
    on the earth.

THEY THINK ME UNWORTHY

They think me unworthy
    my Midé brethren
    but look and see
    the length of my wigwam.

THE SOUND IS FADING AWAY

The sound is fading away
It is of five sounds
    freedom
The sound is fading away
It is of five sounds.

DOCTOR'S SONG

I am singing and dreaming in my poor way
    over the earth
    I who will again disembark
    upon earth.

SONG OF THE TREES

The wind
    only
      I am afraid of.

SONG OF THE THUNDERS

Sometimes
    I go about pitying
    myself
    while I am carried by the wind
    across the sky.

THE APPROACH OF THE STORM

From the half
    of the sky
    that which lives there
    is coming, and makes a noise.

I AM AFRAID OF THE OWL

Very much
    also
    I
    of the owl
    am afraid
    whenever I am sitting alone
      in the wigwam.

I AM AS BRAVE AS OTHER MEN

Men who are brave and heroic

as you esteem them to be
Like them
    I also
    consider myself to be.

MY MUSIC REACHES TO THE SKY

My music
    reaches
    to the sky.

FAREWELL TO THE WARRIORS

Come
    it is time for you to depart
We are going on a long journey.

SONG OF THE MAN WHO WAS TO BE HUNG

The thunders will take me home
    whenever I mind to go home,
    my friends,
    and the wind
    it will take me home, too.

FRIENDLY SONG

I

Over there
    in the sky
    they have taken pity on me.

II

The sky
    loves to hear me.

GAMING SONG
I will go home
    if I am beaten
    after more articles
    to wager.

WAR SONGS
At Co'goben's
    village
    they are weeping
    the men

At Co'goben's
    village
    they are wailing
    the women.

I feel no fear
    when the Great River man
    death
    speaks of.

THE MAN WHO STAYED HOME
Although
    Jinwábe
    considers himself
    a man
    his wife
    certainly
    takes all his attention.

ARROW SONG
Scarlet
    is its head

SONG OF THE BUFFALO
Strike ye
    our land
    with curved horns

SONG OF THE MINISINOWUCK
It is uncertain what will happen
    to the one from whom I fly
It is uncertain what will happen
    to the one from whom I rise.

DRUM SONG
I make them dance
    those brave men
    those brave men
      every one of them.

SONG OF WOMAN-OF-THE-RED-SKY, WHO WENT
WITH HER HUSBAND, SINGING, INTO
BATTLE
At that time
    if I had been a man
    truly
    a man
    I would have seized.

DEATH SONG OF NAMEBINES
The odor of death
I discern the odor of death
    in the front of my body.

THE SIOUX WOMEN GATHER UP THEIR
WOUNDED
The Sioux women
    pass to and fro wailing
    as they gather up
    their wounded men
The voice of their weeping comes back
    to us.

THEY ARE PLAYING A GAME
The noise of passing feet
    on the prairie
They are playing a game as they come
    those men.

SCALP SONG
I wonder
    if she is humiliated
    the Sioux woman
    that I cut off her head.

SONG OF REJOICING
It shall be
    that I rejoice
O, my son

your elder brother
you have brought back
O, my son
it shall be
that I rejoice
O, my son.

DEATH SONG

Is there anyone who
would weep for me?
My wife
would weep for me.

SONG OF THE BUTTERFLY

In the coming heat
of the day
I stood there.

MAPLE SUGAR

Maple sugar
is the only thing
that satisfies me.

A SONG OF SPRING

As my eyes
search
the prairie
I feel the summer in the spring.

CARRIED AROUND THE SKY
As the wind is carrying me
around the sky.

THE SKY WILL RESOUND
It will resound finely
the sky
when I come making a noise.

AN OVERHANGING CLOUD
An overhanging
cloud
repeats my words with pleasing sound.

HEAPS OF CLOUDS
Great heaps
of clouds
in the direction I am looking.

THE NOISE OF THE VILLAGE
Whenever I pause
the noise
of the village.

MIDE BURIAL SONG
Neniwá
let us stand
and you shall see
my body
as I desire.

LOVE SONGS

MY LOVE HAS DEPARTED

I

A loon
    I thought it was
    but it was
    my love's
    splashing oar.

II

To Sault Ste. Marie
    he has departed
My love has gone on before me,
Never again
    can I see him.

THE GENEROUS ONE

Why should
    I, even I
    be jealous
    because of that bad boy?

RECOVERY

Do not weep
I am not going to die.

LOVE-HURT

Although he said it
    still

I am filled with longing
when I think of him.

GLAD-PARTING

Come
    I am going away
I pray you
    let me go
I will soon return
Do not
    weep for me
Behold
    we will be very glad
    to meet each other
    when I return
Do not
    weep for me.

INVITATION

My sweetheart
    a long time
    I have been waiting for you
    to come over
    where I am.

YOU DESIRE VAINLY

You desire vainly
    that I seek you
    the reason is
    I come
    to see your younger sister.

HE IS GONE
I might grieve
I am sad
    that he has gone
    my lover.

SONG OF AN AMBITIOUS MOTHER
    I am asking for
        Bugac's
        daughter
    My big
        brass kettle
        he is giving.

NONSENSE SONG OF THE GAME OF SILENCE
(*If you speak or laugh you are defeated*)
It is hanging
    in the edge of the sunshine
It is a pig I see
    with its double (cloven) hoofs
It is a very fat pig.
The people who live in a hollow tree
    are fighting
They are fighting bloodily
He is rich
He will carry a pack toward the great
    water.
        (*The rabbit speaks*)
At the end of the point of land
I eat the bark off the tree

I see the track of a lynx
I don't care, I can get away from him
It is a jumping trail
    sep!

WORK STEADILY

Be very careful
   to work steadily
I am afraid they will take you away from
    me.

I HAVE FOUND MY LOVER

  Oh
     I am thinking
  Oh
     I am thinking
     I have found
     my lover
  Oh
     I think it is so.

MIDÉ SONGS

*These represent the expression of
religious ideas*

I

  Is it that
    which my voice resembles?
  Even metal
    the sounding of my voice?

II

From beneath the high hill
  my voice echoes forth.

III

The strength of metal
    has entered into my arrow point.
A spirit
    I could kill.
The strength of iron
    has entered into my arrow point.

IV

Beautiful as a star hanging in the sky
    is our Midé lodge.

V

I have gained such spirit-power
    that I can tame it in my hand
It is true
    even our white shell
    I can tame it in my hand.

VI

Do not speak ill of the Midé
    my Midé brethren.
Wherever you may be
    do not speak ill of a woman
    my Midé brethren.

VII

We may live by it always
    my Midé brethren
It is spiritual
    the inspiration we receive.

VIII

In the middle of the sea
    in the lengthy room of the sea
    there I am standing.

IX

I that hasten around
I shoot at a man and he falls in a trance
Then I feel with my hand
    to see if he is still alive.

X

My Midé brother
    is searched
In his heart is found
    that which I seek to remove
    a white shell.

XI

Into thy body
    I shoot
    the spirit

XII

What is this
    I promise you?
The skies shall be bright and clear for you
This is what I promise you.

MEMORIAL ODE

Chief John Buck, hereditary Keeper of the
Wampum, made and sung his ode in 1884 on the
occasion of the removal of the bones of Chief
Red Jacket from their original burying place to
Forest Lawn Cemetery.   The Great League is
the League of the five Iroquois nations in West-
ern New York.

Chant

Now, listen, Ye who established the Great
    League,
Now it has become old,
Now there is nothing but wilderness.

Ye are in your graves who established it.
Ye have taken it with you and have placed
    it under you,
And there is nothing left but desert.
There you have taken your great minds.
That which you established, you have taken
    with you

Ye have placed under your heads what ye
    have established,
The Great League.

Refrain

Woe, Woe! Hearken ye!
  We are diminished
Woe, woe!
  The land has become a thicket.
Woe, woe!
  The clear places are deserted
  They are in their graves who established
    it.
Woe, the Great League!
  Yet they declared it should endure.
The Great League, Woe!
  Their work has grown old
  We are become wretched. Woe!

SONGS FROM THE SOUTHEAST

FRAGMENT FROM THE WALLUM-OLUM OR CHRONICLE OF THE LENI-LENÂPÉ

(Delaware)

After the rushing waters had subsided
The Lenâpé of the Turtle were close to-
    gether,
In hollow houses, living together there.
It freezes where they abode:
It snows where they abode:
It storms where they abode:
It is cold where they abode.
At this northern place they speak favor-
    ably
Of mild, cool lands
With many deer and buffaloes.
As they journeyed, some being strong,
Some being rich, they separated
Into house-builders and hunters:
The hunters showed themselves at the
    north:
The hunters showed themselves at the east:
The hunters showed themselves at the
    south:
The hunters showed themselves at the west.

In that ancient country, in that northern
country,
In that Turtle country
The best of Lenâpé were the Turtle-men.
All the cabin fires of that land were dis-
quieted
And all said, "Let us go."
To the Snake land, to the east, they went
Going away, earnestly grieving.
Split asunder, weak, trembling, their land
burned
They went, torn and broken, to Snake
Island.
Those from the north being free, without
care
Went forth from the land of snow in dif-
ferent directions.
The fathers of the Bald Eagle and the
White Wolf remain
Along the sea, rich in fish and strength.
Floating up stream in their canoes
Our fathers were rich, they were in the
light
When they were at those islands.
Head Beaver and Big Bird said:
"Let us go to Snake Island," they said.
All say they will go along
To destroy all the land.
Those of the north agreed,
Those of the east agreed,

Over the sea, the frozen sea,
They went to enjoy it.
On the wonderful slippery water,
On the stone-hard water all went,
On the great tidal sea, the muscle-bearing
    sea.
Ten thousand at night,
All in one night,
To the Snake Island, to the east, at night,
They walk and walk, all of them.
The men from the north, the east, the
    south:
The Eagle clan, the Beaver clan, the Wolf
    clan,
The best men, the rich men, the head men,
Those with wives, those with daughters,
    those with dogs.
They all come, they tarry at the land of the
    spruce-pines:
Those from the west come without hesi-
    tation,
Esteeming highly their old home at the
    Turtle land.
There was no rain and no corn
So they moved further seaward.
At the place of caves, in the Buffalo land,
They at last had food on a pleasant plain.

NOTE.—This famous fragment, the only written (pic-
tograph) historical record extant among the Eastern
tribes, is included as an example of the Saga element
in Indian literature.

SACRED FORMULAS OF THE CHEROKEES

I

CONCERNING LIVING HUMANITY
(*Love Charm*)

Hû! Listen! In Alahí yi you repose, O
    Terrible Woman,
O you have drawn near to hearken.
There in Elahiyi you are at rest, a White
    Woman.
No one is ever lonely when with you.
You are most beautiful.
Instantly and at once you have rendered
    me a white man.
No one is ever lonely when with me.
Now you have made the path white for me.
It shall never be dreary.
Now you have put me into it.
It shall never become blue.
You have brought down to me from above
    the white road.
There in mid-earth you have placed me.
I shall stand erect upon the earth.
No one is ever lonely when with me.

NOTE.—White—happy; blue—despondent. "To make
lonely" or to be "lonely" was, to the Cherokees, the
depth of degradation.

I am very handsome.
You have put me into the white house.
I shall be in it as it moves about and no
    one with me shall ever be lonely.
Verily, I shall never become blue.
Instantly you have caused it to be so with
    me.

And now there in Elahiyi you have ren-
    dered the woman blue.
Now you have made the path blue for her.
Let her be completely veiled in loneliness.
Put her into the blue road.
And now bring her down.
  Place her standing upon the earth.
  Where her feet are now and wherever she
    may go, let loneliness leave its mark
    upon her.
Let her be marked out for loneliness where
    she stands.

Ha! I belong to the Wolf clan, that one
    alone which was allotted into for you.
No one is ever lonely with me.
I am handsome.
Let her put her soul in the very center of
    my soul, never to turn away.
Grant that, in the midst of men she shall
    never think of them.

I belong to the one clan alone which was
allotted for you when the seven clans
were established.

Where other men live it is lonely.
They are very loathsome.
The common polecat has made them so like
himself that they are fit only for his
company.
They have become mere refuse.
They are very loathsome.
The common opossum has made them so
like himself that they are fit only to
be with him.
They are very loathsome.
Even the crow has made them so like him-
self that they are fit only for his
company.
They are very loathsome.
The miserable rain-crow has made them so
like himself that they are fit only for
his company.

The seven clans all alike make one feel very
lonely in their company.
They are not even good looking.
They go about clothed with mere refuse.
They even go about covered with dung.
But I—I was ordained to be a white man.

I stand with my face toward the Sun Land.
No one is ever lonely with me.
I am very handsome.
I shall certainly never become blue.
I am covered by the everlasting white
    house wherever I go.
No one is ever lonely with me.
Your soul has come into the center of my
    soul, never to turn away.
I, Gatigwan asti—I take your soul.
Sge!

II

TO INSURE CONSTANCY

Listen! O, now you have drawn near to
    hearken, O, Ancient One.
This woman's soul has come to rest at the
    edge of your body.
You are never to let go your hold upon it.
It is ordained that you shall do just as you
    are requested to do.
Let her never think upon any other place.
Her soul has faded within her.
She is bound by the black threads.

III

Listen! "Ha! Now the souls have met,
    never to part," you have said, O An-
    cient One above.

O Black Spider, you have brought down
from on high.
You have let down your web.
She is of the Deer clan; her name is
Ayâsta.
Her soul you have wrapped up in your web.

Listen! Ha! But now you have covered her
with loneliness.
Her eyes have faded.
Whither can her soul escape?
Let her be sorrowing as she goes along,
and not for one night alone.
Let her become an aimless wanderer, whose
trail may never be followed.
O Black Spider, may you hold her soul in
your web so that it shall never get
through the meshes.
What is the name of the soul?
They two have come together.
It is mine!

Listen! Ha! And now you have hearkened,
O Ancient Red.
Your grandchildren have come to the edge
of your body.
You hold them yet more firmly in your
grasp, never to let go your hold.
O Ancient One, we have become as one.
The woman has put her soul into our
hands.

We shall never let it go!
Yu!

IV
TO DESTROY LIFE

Listen! Now I have come to step over your
  soul.
You are of the Wolf clan.
Your name is A'yû'nini.
Your spittle I have put at rest under the
  earth.
I have come to cover you over with the
  black rock.
I have come to cover you over with the
  black cloth.
I have come to cover you over with the
  black slabs, never to reappear.
Toward the black coffin of the upland in
  the Darkening Land your paths shall
  stretch out.
So shall it be for you.
The clay of the upland has come to cover
  you.
Instantly the black clay has lodged there
  where it is at rest at the black houses
  in the Darkening Land.
With the black coffin and with the black
  slabs I have come to cover you.
Now your soul has faded away.
It has become blue.

When darkness comes your spirit shall
grow less and dwindle away, never to
reappear.
Listen!

V

THOSE ABOUT TO BE SLAIN

Ha yi! Yû! Listen!
Now instantly we have lifted up the red
war club.
Quickly his soul shall be without motion.
There under the earth, where the black
war clubs shall be moving about like
ball sticks in the game, there his soul
shall be, never to reappear.
We cause it to be so.
He shall never go and lift up the war club.
We cause it to be so.
There under the earth the black war club
and the black fog have come together
as one for their covering.
The black fog shall never be lifted from
them.
We cause it to be so.

SONGS FROM THE
GREAT PLAINS

HUNTING SONGS
(*Dakota*)

I

Something I've killed, and I lift up my
    voice;
Something I've killed, and I lift up my
    voice;
The northern buffalo I've killed, and I
    lift up my voice;
Something I've killed, and I lift up my
    voice.

II

The saddle bind:
Children dear.
For half a day,
I will kill.

THE FASHIONING OF THE CHIL-
DREN
(*Osage*)

CHANT OF THE RED EAGLE CLAN

The First of the Race
Was saying, "Ho, younger brother! the
    children have no bodies.

47

"We shall seek bodies for our children.

"Ho, younger brother! you shall attend
to it."

They reached one upper world and stood.

There they were not human beings.

"Ho, younger brother! the children have
no bodies," he was saying.

"We must seek bodies for our children."

They reached the second upper world and
stood.

There they were not human beings.

"Ho, younger brother! the children have
no bodies," he was saying.

"We must seek bodies for our children."

They reached the third upper world and
stood.

There they were not human beings.

"Ho, younger brother! the children have
no bodies," he was saying.

"We must seek bodies for our children."

They reached the fourth upper world and
stood.

There they became human beings.

Still, the children were without (human)
bodies.

"We must continue to seek bodies for our
children."

They returned to the third upper world
and stood.

The children were really without bodies.

"Ho, younger brother! the children have
　　no bodies," he was saying.

"We must continue to seek bodies for our
　　children."

They returned to the second upper world
　　and stood.

The children did not find bodies for them-
　　selves.

"Ho, younger brother! the children have
　　no bodies," he was saying.

"We must make an examination awhile
　　longer."

They returned to the first upper world and
　　stood.

They came to red oak and were standing
　　on it.

On a very fine day they came hither and
　　stood.

Kaxe-wahü-sa (the Black Bear), who was
　　then moving,

Came directly to them and stood.

"Ho, elder brother!" (said the Black
　　Bear.)

"You shall continue to burn my feet for
　　me."

"Ho, Kaxe-wahü-sa!" was he (the Tsicu)
　　saying.

Kaxe-wahü-sa went to the star Watse-
　　tuka.

"Ho, grandfather!" he was saying.

"The children have no bodies."

Watse-tuka replied, "Can I give the children bodies?

"I have an everlasting road in which I must keep.

"I am not the only mysterious one;

"You shall attend to it awhile longer."

Then Kaxe-wahü-sa went to the star Watse-mika.

"Ho, grandmother!" he said;

"The children have no bodies."

She replied, "Can I give bodies to the children?

"I have an everlasting road in which I must keep.

"I am not the only mysterious one!

"You shall attend to it awhile longer."

Then he went to the mysterious one of day.

"Ho, grandfather!" said he;

"The children have no bodies."

Said he, "Can I give the children bodies?

"I have an everlasting road in which I must keep.

"I am not the only mysterious one;

"You shall attend to it awhile longer."

Then he went to the mysterious one of night.

"Ho, grandfather!" said he;

"The children have no bodies, grandfather!"

The Moon replied, "Can I give bodies to
    the children?
"I have an everlasting road in which I
    must keep.
"I am not the only mysterious one;
"You shall attend to it awhile longer."
Then he went to the Pleiades, saying,
"Ho, grandfathers!
"The children have no bodies."
One of these replied, "Can I give bodies
    to the children!
"I have an everlasting road in which I
    must keep.
"I am not the only mysterious one;
"You shall attend to it awhile longer."
Then he went to the constellation called
    Three Deer.
"Ho, grandfather," said he;
"The children have no bodies."
The latter replied, "Can I give the chil-
    dren bodies?
"I have an everlasting road in which I
    must keep.
"I am not the only mysterious one;
"You shall attend to it awhile longer."
Then he went to the Morning Star, saying,
"Ho, grandfather!
"The children have no bodies."
The star replied, "Can I give bodies to the
    children?

"I have an everlasting road in which I
must keep.

"I am not the only mysterious one;

"You shall attend to it awhile longer."

Then he went to the Small Star, saying,

"Ho, grandfather!

"The children have no bodies."

The star replied, "Can I give bodies to the
children?

"I have an everlasting road in which I
must keep.

"I am not the only mysterious one;

"You shall attend to it awhile longer."

The female Red Bird, who had been mov-
ing, was sitting on her nest.

To her he came, saying,

"Ho, grandmother!

"The children have no bodies."

She replied, "I can cause your children to
have (human) bodies from my own.

"My left wing shall be a left arm for the
children.

"My right wing shall be a right arm for
them.

"My head shall be a head for them.

"My mouth shall be a mouth for them.

"My forehead shall be a forehead for
them.

"My neck shall be a neck for them.

"My throat shall be a throat for them.

"My chest shall be a chest for them.
"My thighs shall be thighs for them.
"My knees shall be knees for them.
"My heels shall be their heels.
"My toes shall be their toes.
"My claws shall be their toenails.
"You shall live forever without destruc-
    tion.
"Your children shall live as human beings.
"The speech of children I will bestow on
    your children."

THE CHILD IS INTRODUCED TO THE
COSMOS AT BIRTH

(*Omaha*)

Ho! Ye Sun, Moon, Stars, all ye that
    move in the heavens,
  I bid you hear me!
Into your midst has come a new life.
    Consent ye, I implore!
Make its path smooth, that it may reach
    the brow of the first hill!

Ho! Ye Winds, Clouds, Rain, Mist, all ye
    that move in the air,
  I bid you hear me!
Into your midst has come a new life.
    Consent ye, I implore!

Make its path smooth, that it may reach
    the brow of the second hill!
Ho! Ye Hills, Valleys, Rivers, Lakes,
    Trees, Grasses, all ye of the earth,
    I bid you hear me!
Into your midst has come a new life.
    Consent ye, I implore!
Make its path smooth, that it may reach
    the brow of the third hill!
Ho! Ye Birds, great and small, that fly
    in the air,
Ho! Ye Animals, great and small, that
    dwell in the forest,
Ho! Ye insects that creep among the
    grasses and burrow in the ground—
    I bid you hear me!
Into your midst has come a new life.
    Consent ye, I implore!
Make its path smooth, that it may reach the
    brow of the fourth hill!

Ho! All ye of the heavens, all ye of the
    air, all ye of the earth:
    I bid you all to hear me!
Into your midst has come a new life.
    Consent ye, consent ye all, I implore!
Make its path smooth—then shall it travel
    beyond the four hills!

RITUAL CHANT AT THE PREPARA-
TION OF THE SWEAT LODGE
FOR THE SICK
(*Omaha*)

The Stone, with the curative powers of its heat, becomes a symbol of permanency and strength.

Ho! Aged One, eçka,
At a time when there were gathered to-
    gether seven persons,
You sat in the seventh place, it is said,
And of the Seven you alone possessed
    knowledge of all things,
    Aged One, eçka.
When in their longing for protection and
    guidance,
The people sought in their minds for a
    way,
They beheld you sitting with assured per-
    manency and endurance
In the center where converged the paths,
There, exposed to the violence of the four
    winds, you sat,
Possessed with power to receive supplica-
    tions,
    Aged One, eçka.
Where is his mouth, by which there may be
    utterance of speech?
Where is his heart, to which there may
    come knowledge and understanding?

NOTE.—Eçka—I implore.

Where are his feet, whereby he may move
    from place to place?
We question in wonder,
Yet verily it is said you alone have power
    to receive supplications,
    Aged One, eçka.
I have desired to go yet farther in the path
    of life with my little ones,
Without pain, without sickness,
Beyond the second, third, and fourth pe-
    riod of life's pathway,
    Aged One, eçka.
O hear! This is my prayer,
Although uttered in words poorly put to-
    gether,
    Aged One, eçka.

RITUAL CHANT FOR THE SICK
(Omaha)

He! Aged One, eçka
Thou Rock, eçka
Aged One, eçka
He! I have taught these little ones
They obey, eçka
Aged One, eçka
He!
He! Unmoved from time without end, ver-
    ily
Thou sittest, eçka

In the midst of the various paths of the
    coming winds
In the midst of the winds thou sittest,
    eçka
Aged One, eçka
He! The small grasses grow about thee,
    eçka
Thou sittest as though making of them thy
    dwelling place, eçka
He! Verily thou sittest covered with the
    droppings of birds, eçka
Thy head decked with the downy feathers
    of the birds, eçka
Aged One, eçka
Thou who standest next in power, eçka
He! thou water, eçka
Water that hast been flowing
From time unknown, eçka
He! Of you the little ones have taken
Though thy mysteries remain unrevealed
These little ones crave thy touch, eçka
He! Thou that standest as one dwelling
    place, eçka
Even as one dwelling place, eçka
Ye great animals, eçka
He! Who make for us the covering, eçka
These little ones, thou hast said, let their
    thoughts reverently dwell on me, eçka
He! Thou tent frame, eçka

Thou standest with bent back o'er us
With stooping shoulders, bending over us
Verily, thou standest
Thus my little ones shall speak of me, thou
    hast said
Brushing back the hair from thy forehead,
    eçka
The hair of thy head
The grass that grows about thee
Thy hairs are whitened, eçka
The hairs that grow upon thy head, eçka
O, the paths that the little ones shall take,
    eçka
Whichever way they may flee from danger,
    eçka
They shall escape. Their shoulders shall
    be bent with age as they walk
As they walk on the well-beaten path
Shading their brows now and again with
    their hands
As they walk in their old age, eçka
That of thy strength they shall partake,
    eçka
Therefore thy little ones desire to walk
    closely by thy side, eçka
Venerable One, eçka.

RITUAL OF THE COSMIC FORCES
(Omaha)

Toward the coming of the sun

There the people of every kind gathered,
And great animals of every kind.
Verily all gathered together, as well as
    people.
Insects also of every description,
Verily all gathered there together,
By what means or manner we know not.
Verily, one alone of all these was the
    greatest,
Inspiring to all minds,
The great white rock,
Standing and reaching as high as the heav-
    ens, enwrapped in mist,
Verily as high as the heavens.
Thus my little ones shall speak of me,
As long as they shall travel in life's path,
    thus they shall speak of me.
Such was the words, it has been said.
Then next in rank
Thou, male of the crane, stoodst with thy
    long beak
And thy neck, none like to it in length,
There with thy beak didst thou strike the
    earth.

*   *   *   *   *   *   *

This shall be the legend
Of the people of yore, the red people,
Thus my little ones shall speak of me.

Then next in rank stood the male gray
 wolf, whose cry,
Though uttered without effort, verily made
 the earth to tremble,
Even the stable earth to tremble.
Such shall be the legend of the people.
Then next in rank stood Hega, the buzzard,
 with his red neck.
Calmly he stood, his great wings spread,
 letting the heat of the sun straighten
 his feathers.
Slowly he flapped his wings,
Then floated away, as though without ef-
 fort,
Thus displaying a power (a gift of Wakon-
 da) often to be spoken of by the old
 men in their teachings.

SONG OF SCORN
(Omaha)

Ena! The one I wish to marry has gone
 to war.
Ena! The one I hate has not gone forth
 but remains here.

THE GHOST-DANCE RELIGION

In 1892 the last serious Indian outbreak occurred. This was occasioned by the government's efforts to suppress the practices of a new religion which, during the two years preceding, had spread over a large part of the west, among the Indian tribes from the Plains to the Coast, and from the Columbia to the Rio Grande. The Prophet of this new cult claimed to be the Messiah, and professed to exercise divine powers. He instituted certain dances, which his followers, in a vain attempt to overthrow the world-order magically, perverted into frenzied rites, wherein entranced, they saw visions and spoke with the dead. The Messiah concept is an ancient one in Indian mythology, antedating all Christian influence, and so desperate had become the straits of the Vanishing Race that these doctrines received wide acceptance. At length the government intervened and brought the strange worship to an end.

Mr. James Mooney investigated this interesting phenomenon and actually discovered the Seer, who proved to be an inoffensive visionary dwelling in a remote valley of the Southwest. This young man's life and theories (a full-blood, apparently untouched by Christian influence), curiously resembled those of Christ, and like the latter, he preached the doctrines of Non-resistance and the Brotherhood of Man. In this case our government played the part of Rome.

These songs were sung during the dancing, and express in the image of the Whirlwind, a mystic and exalted contemplation of the approaching Great Change. Unessential repetitions have been omitted for brevity's sake.

SONGS OF THE GHOST-DANCE RELIGION
(*Arapaho*)

DISILLUSION

I

My children, when at first I liked the
    Whites,
My children, when at first I liked the
    Whites,
I gave them fruits,
I gave them fruits.

ECSTASY

II

My children, my children,
The wind makes the head-feathers sing—
The wind makes the head-feathers sing.
My children, my children.

LABORS OF THE SPIRIT

III

My children, my children,
I take pity on those who have been taught,

Because they push on hard,
Says our Father.

WONDER
IV
How bright is the moonlight!
Tonight as I ride with my load of buffalo
    beef.

THE WHIRLWIND (POWER OF CHANGE) SPEAKS
V
I circle around
The boundaries of earth,
Wearing the long wing feathers as I fly.

VISION
VI
My children, my children,
Look! the earth is about to move.
My Father tells me so.

SPIRIT-JOY
VII
I fly around yellow,
I fly with the wild rose on my head,
On high—He'e'e'!

REVELATION
VIII
My children, my children,
It is I who wear the morning star on my
    head;
I show it to my children,
Says the Father.

TRAVAIL OF SPIRIT
IX

Father, have pity on me,
Father, have pity on me;
I am crying for thirst;
All is gone—I have nothing to eat.

INVOCATION
IX

Father, the Morning Star!
Father, the Morning Star!
Look on us, we have danced until daylight,
Take pity on us—Hi'i'i!

THE MESSIAH SPEAKS
(*Cheyenne*)

I am coming in sight—
I bring the Whirlwind with me—
That you may know one another.

REINCARNATION
(*Comanche*)

We shall live again,
We shall live again.
The sun's beams are spreading out—
    He'e'yo'!
The sun's yellow rays are spreading out—
    Ahi'ni'yo'!

SONGS OF LIFE RETURNING
(*Paiute*)

I

The wind stirs the willows.
The wind stirs the grasses.

II

The cottonwoods are growing tall,
They are growing tall and verdant.

III

A slender antelope,
A slender antelope
He is wallowing upon the ground.

IV

Fog! Fog!
Lightning! Lightning!
Whirlwind! Whirlwind!

V

Whirlwind! Whirlwind!
The snowy earth comes gliding, the snowy
    earth comes gliding.

VI

There is dust from the whirlwind,
There is dust from the whirlwind,
The whirlwind on the mountain.

VII

The rocks are ringing,
The rocks are ringing,
They are ringing in the mountains.

SONG OF THE PATH OF SOULS
VIII

The snow lies there—ro'rani!
The snow lies there—ro'rani!
The milky way lies there!

CREATION
(Sioux)

I

This is my work—Yo'yoyo'!
All that grows upon the earth is mine—
    Yo'yoyo'!
Says the Father—Yo'yoyo'!
E'ya Yo'yoyo'!

LAMENT
II

Mother, come home; mother, come home.
My little brother goes about always crying,
My little brother goes about always crying.
Mother, come home; mother come home.

COURIER CHANT
III

He! They have come back racing,

Why, they say there is to be a buffalo hunt
    over here,
Why, they say there is to be a buffalo hunt
    over here,
Make arrows! Make arrows!
Says the Father, says the Father,

THE MILLENIUM

IV

The whole world is coming,
A nation is coming, a nation is coming,
The Eagle has brought the message to the
    tribe.
Over the whole earth they are coming;
The buffalo are coming, the buffalo are
    coming,
The Crow has brought the message to the
    tribe.

JUDGMENT

(*Kiowa*)

I

The Father will descend.
Everybody will arise.
Stretch out your hands.
The earth will tremble.

VISITATION

II

The spirit army is approaching,
The whole world is moving onward.
See! Everybody is standing watching.
Let us all pray.

THE SECRET OF HUMANITY

III

Because I am poor,
I pray for every living creature.

THE GOD-MAN

IV

My Father has had pity on me.
I have eyes like my Father's,
I have hands like my Father's,
I have legs like my Father's,
I have a form like my Father's.

THE SPIRIT HUNTERS

V

The spirit host is advancing, they say.
They are coming with the buffalo, they say.
They are coming with the new earth, they
    say.

MYSTIC

VI

That wind, that wind
Shakes my tipi, shakes my tipi,
And sings a song for me,
And sings a song for me.

EXHORTATION

(*Caddo*)

Come on, Caddo, we are all going up,
Co on, Caddo, we are all going up
To the great village—He'e'ye'!

To the great village—He'e'ye'!
With our Father above,
With our Father above when he dwells
    on high—He'e'ye'!
Where our Mother dwells—Hhe'e'ye'!
Where our Mother dwells—Hhe'e'ye'!

SONGS FROM THE SOUTHWEST

VIRACOCHA
(*Ancient Inca*)

Beautiful Princess
Lo, thy ·brother
Breaks thy vessel
Now in fragments.
From the blow comes
Thunder, lightning,
Strokes of lightning.
And thou, princess,
Take the water;
As the rain, fall;
As the hail, fall;
As the snow, fall;
Viracocha
World-dispensor.

WAR SONGS
(*Zuñi*)

To you of the six regions
Whose homes cover the earth
I give shells.
Yellow ant, blue ant, red ant, all color ant
U—hu—we—u—hu—we—
U—hu—we—u—hu—we.

73

To you whose homes
Are covered with mountain tops
I give shells
Yellow, blue, red, white, all color, black.
When we meet the enemy
A little arrow storm will arise.
When we meet him on the road near by
He will never more inhale the sacred
    breath of day.
I inhale the sacred breath of day.
All come quickly,
The enemy comes from ambush.
A Navajo is killed,
We inhale the sacred breath of day.

You have met the enemy.
He will never more inhale the sacred
    breath of day.
The enemy is destroyed.
Who will be our great Bow priest?
Who is to become a Bow priest?
Well! who will kick the scalp?
His younger mother, his elder sister.
Who will wash the scalp?
His younger father, his elder brother.
Well!
Good!

PRAYER FOR RAIN
(*Sia*)

White floating clouds,

Clouds like the plains
Come and water the earth.
Sun embrace the earth
That she may be fruitful.
Moon, lion of the north,
Bear of the west,
Badger of the south,
Wolf of the east,
Eagle of the heavens,
Shrew of the earth,
Elder war hero,
Warriors of the six mountains of the
    world,
Intercede with the cloud people for us,
That they may water the earth.
Medicine bowl, cloud bowl, and water vase
Give us your hearts,
That the earth may be watered.
I make the ancient road of meal,
That my song may pass over it—
The ancient road.
White shell bead woman
Who lives where the sun goes down,
Mother Whirlwind,
Father Sus'sistinnako,
Mother Ya'ya, creator of good thoughts.
Yellow woman of the north,
Blue woman of the west,
Red woman of the south,
White woman of the east,

Slightly yellow woman of the zenith,
And dark woman of the nadir,
I ask your intercession with the cloud
    people.

RAIN SONG OF THE GIANT SOCIETY
(*Sia*)

We, the Ancient Ones,
Who ascended from the middle of the
    world below,
Our medicine is precious,
It is as our hearts precious to us,
Arrow of lightning
Come to us
Echo.
Spruce of the north
And all your people;
Your thoughts come to us.
Who is it?
White floating clouds.
May your thoughts come to us
And all your people,
May their thoughts come to us.
Who is it?
Clouds like the plains,
May your thoughts come to us.
Who is it?
Arrow of lightning,
May your thoughts come to us.
Who is it?

Earth horizon
And all your people,
May your thoughts come to us.

INVOCATION TO THE U'WANNAMI
(*Sia*)

I

Come you, ascend the ladder; all come in;
    all sit down.
We were poor, poor, poor, poor, poor, poor,
When we came to this world through the
    poor place,
Where the body of water dried for our
    passing.
Banked up clouds cover the earth.
All come four times with your showers,
Descend to the base of the ladder and
    stand still;
Bring your showers and great rains.
All, all come, all ascend, all come in, all
    sit down.

II

I throw out to you my sacred meal that you
    may all come.
Hold your gaming-stick; throw it forward;
    all come.
All come out and give us your showers and
    great rains; all come,

That the seeds may be strong and come up,
that all seed plants may come up and
be strong.

Come you that all trees and seeds may
come up and be strong.

Come you hither; all come.

III

Cover my earth mother four times with
many flowers.

Let the heavens be covered with the banked
up clouds.

Let the earth be covered with fog; cover
the earth with rains.

Great waters, rains, cover the earth.
Lightning cover the earth.

Let thunder be heard over the earth; let
thunder be heard;

Let thunder be heard over the six regions
of the earth.

IV

Rain-makers, come out from all roads that
great rivers may cover the earth;

That stones may be moved by the torrents;

That trees may be uprooted and moved by
the torrents.

Great rain-makers, come out from all
roads, carry the sands of our earth
mother of the place.

Cover the earth with her heart, that all
seeds may develop,

That my children may have all things to
    eat and be happy;
That the people of the outlying villages
    may all laugh and be happy;
That the growing children may all have
    things to eat and be happy.
This way our great father wishes you to
    come.
This way our great mother wishes you to
    come.
That we may have all kinds of seeds and
    all things good;
That we may inhale the sacred breath of
    life;
That our fathers and our mothers may
    bring us happy days.
Let our children live and be happy.
Send us the good south winds.
Send us your breath over the lakes that
    our great world may be made beauti-
    ful and our people may live.

V

There, far off, my Sun Father arises, as-
    cends the ladder, comes forth from his
    place.
May all complete the road of life, may all
    grow old.
May the children inhale more of the sacred
    breath of life.

May all my children have corn that they
may complete the road of life.

Here sit down; here remain; we give you
our best thoughts.

Hasten over the meal road; we are jealous
of you.

We inhale the sacred breath through our
prayer plumes.

MAGPIE SONG
(Navajo)

The Magpie! The Magpie! Here under-
neath

In the white of his wings are the footsteps
of morning.

It dawns! It dawns!

SONGS IN THE GARDEN OF THE
HOUSE GOD
(Navajo)

I

Truly in the East
The white bean
And the great corn-plant
Are tied with the white lightning.
Listen! rain approaches!
The voice of the bluebird is heard.
Truly in the East
The white bean
And the great squash
Are tied with the rainbow,

Listen! rain approaches!
The voice of the bluebird is heard.

II

From the top of the great corn-plant the
    water gurgles, I hear it;
Around the roots the water foams, I hear
    it;
Around the roots of the plants it foams, I
    hear it;
From their tops the water foams, I hear it.

III

The corn grows up. The waters of the
    dark clouds drop, drop.
The rain descends. The waters from the
    corn leaves drop, drop.
The rain descends. The waters from the
    plants drop, drop.
The corn grows up. The waters of the
    dark mists drop, drop.

IV

Shall I cull this fruit of the great corn-
    plant?
Shall you break it? Shall I break it?
Shall I break it? Shall you break it?
Shall I? Shall you?
Shall I cull this fruit of the great squash
    vine?
Shall you pick it up? Shall I pick it up?
Shall I pick it up? Shall you pick it up?
Shall I? Shall you?

THE MOUNTAIN CHANT OF THE NAVAJO

CHARACTER OF THE SONGS

Some songs are self-explanatory or readily understood, but the greater number cannot be comprehended without a full knowledge of the mythology and of the symbolism to which they refer; they merely hint at mythic conceptions. Many contain archaic expressions, for which the shaman can assign a meaning, but whose etymology cannot now be learned; and some embody obsolete words whose meaning is lost even to the priesthood. There are many vocables known to be meaningless and recited merely to fill out the rhythm or to give a dignified length to the song. For the same reasons a meaningless syllable is often added or a significant syllable duplicated.

Other poetical licenses are taken, such as the omission of a syllable, the change of accent, the substitution of one vowel for another. The most familiar words are often distorted beyond recognition. For these various reasons the task of noting and translating these songs is one of considerable difficulty. In order to simplify the meaning of certain chants repetative phrases are set as refrains.

PRELUDE

INVOCATION TO DSILYI N'EYANI

Reared Within the Mountains!
Lord of the Mountains!
Young Man!
Chieftain!
I have made your sacrifice.
I have prepared a smoke for you.
My feet restore thou for me.
My legs restore thou for me.

My body restore thou for me.
My mind restore thou for me.
My voice restore thou for me.
Restore all for me in beauty.
Make beautiful all that is before me.
Make beautiful all that is behind me.
It is done in beauty.
It is done in beauty.
It is done in beauty.
It is done in beauty.

FIRST SONG OF THE THUNDER

Thonah! Thonah!
There is a voice above,
The voice of the thunder.
Within the dark cloud,
Again and again it sounds,
Thonah! Thonah!
Thonah! Thonah!
There is a voice below,
The voice of the grasshopper.
Among the plants,
Again and again it sounds,
Thonah! Thonah!

II

TWELFTH SONG OF THE THUNDER

The voice that beautifies the land!
The voice above,
The voice of the thunder
Within the dark cloud
Again and again it sounds,

The voice that beautifies the land!
The voice that beautifies the land!
The voice below;
The voice of the grasshopper
Among the plants .
Again and again it sounds,
The voice that beautifies the land!

III

FIRST SONG OF THE EXPLODING STICK

Young Woman Who Becomes a Bear set
    fire in the mountains
In many places; as she journeyed on
There was a line of burning mountains.
The Otter set fire in the waters
In many places; as he journeyed on
There was a line of burning waters.

IV

LAST SONG OF THE EXPLODING STICK

Maid Who Becomes a Bear sought the gods
    and found them;
On the high mountain peaks she sought the
    gods and found them;
Truly with my sacrifice she sought the
    gods and found them.
Somebody doubts it, so I have heard.

V

FIRST DAYLIGHT SONG

The curtain of daybreak is hanging,
The Daylight Boy (it is hanging),
From the land of day it is hanging;

Before him, as it dawns, it is hanging;
Behind him, as it dawns, it is hanging.
Before him, in beauty, it is hanging;
Behind him, in beauty, it is hanging;
From his voice, in beauty, it is hanging.

VI

LAST DAYLIGHT SONG

Lullaby, lullaby.
It is daybreak. Lullaby.
Now comes the Daylight Boy. Lullaby.
Now it is day. Lullaby.
Now comes the Daylight Girl. Lullaby.

VII

SONG OF THE PROPHET

That flowing water! That flowing water!
My mind wanders across it.
That broad water! That flowing water!
My mind wanders across it.
That old age water! That flowing water!
My mind wanders across it.

VIII

SONG OF THE RISING SUN DANCE

Where the sun rises,
The Holy Young Man
The great plumed arrow
Has swallowed
And withdrawn it.
The sun
Is satisfied.
Where the sun sets,

The Holy Young Woman
The cliff rose arrow
Has swallowed
And withdrawn it.
The moon
Is satisfied.

IX

LAST WORDS OF THE PROPHET

Farewell, my younger brother!

From the holy places the gods come for me.

You will never see me again; but when the
showers pass and the thunders peal,

"There," you will say, "is the voice of my
elder brother."

And when the harvest comes, of the beautiful birds and grasshoppers you will
say,

"There is the ordering of my elder
brother!"

SONG OF BÉKOTSIDI WHEN HE MADE THINGS

*Both of the gods sang while they were at work,
and this was the song that Békotsidi sang to bless
all that he was making. It was the first song
which he sang at this work.*

Now Békotsidi, that am I.
   For them I make.
Now child of Day Bearer am I.
   For them I make.

Now Day Bearer's beam of blue.
>   *For them I make.*
Shines on my feet and your feet too.
>   *For them I make.*
Horses of all kinds now increase.
>   *For them I make.*
At my fingers' tips and yours.
>   *For them I make.*
Beasts of all kinds now increase.
>   *For them I make.*
The bluebirds now increase.
>   *For them I make.*
Soft goods of all kinds now increase.
>   *For them I make.*
Now with the pollen they increase.
>   *For them I make.*
Increasing now, they will last forever.
>   *For them I make.*
In old age wandering on the trail of beauty.
>   *For them I make.*
To form them fair, for them I labor.
>   *For them I make.*

SONGS OF DAWN BOY
I

Where my kindred dwell,
>   *There I wander.*
The Red Rock House,
>   *There I wander.*

Where dark kethawns are at the doorway,
> *There I wander.*

With the pollen of dawn upon my trail,
> *There I wander.*

At the yuni, the striped cotton hangs with pollen.
> *There I wander.*

Going around with it.
> *There I wander.*

Taking another, I depart with it.
> *With it I wander.*

In the house of long life,
> *There I wander.*

In the house of happiness,
> *There I wander.*

Beauty before me,
> *With it I wander.*

Beauty behind me,
> *With it I wander.*

Beauty below me,
> *With it I wander.*

Beauty above me,
> *With it I wander.*

Beauty all around me,
> *With it I wander.*

In old age traveling,
> *With it I wander.*

On the beautiful trail I am,
> *With it I wander.*

II

In Kininaéki.
In the house made of dawn.
In the story made of dawn.
On the trail of dawn.
O, Talking God!
His feet, my feet, restore
His limbs, my limbs, restore.
His body, my body, restore.
His mind, my mind, restore.
His voice, my voice, restore.
His plumes, my plumes, restore.
With beauty before him, with beauty before
     me.
With beauty behind him, with beauty be-
     hind me.
With beauty above him, with beauty below
     me.
With beauty below him, with beauty below
     me.
With beauty around him, with beauty
     around me.
With pollen beautiful in his voice, with
     pollen beautiful in my voice.
It is finished in beauty.
It is finished in beauty.
In the house of evening light.
From the story made of evening light.
On the trail of evening light.
O, House God!
     (The rest as in I, except that lines 12 and 13 are
transposed.)

III

To the house of my kindred,
>*There I return.*

Child of the yellow corn am I.

To the Red Rock House,
>*There I return.*

Where the blue kethawns are by the door-
way,
>*There I return.*

The pollen of evening light on my trail,
>*There I return.*

At the yuni the haliotis shell hangs with the
pollen,

Going around,
>*With it I return.*

Taking another, I walk out with it.
>*With it I return.*

To the house of old age,
>*Up there I return.*

To the house of happiness,
>*Up there I return.*

Beauty behind me,
>*With it I return.*

Beauty before me,
>*With it I return.*

Beauty above me,
>*With it I return.*

Beauty below me,
>*With it I return.*

Beauty all around me,
>*With it I return.*
Now in old age wandering,
>*I return.*
Now on the trail of beauty, I am.
>*There I return.*

A PRAYER

(FOR SECOND DAY OF THE NIGHT CHANT)

From the base of the east.
From the base of the Pelado Peak.
From the house made of mirage,
From the story made of mirage,
From the doorway of rainbow,
The path out of which is the rainbow,
The rainbow passed out with me.
The rainbow raised up with me.
Through the middle of broad fields,
The rainbow returned with me.
To where my house is visible,
The rainbow returned with me.
To the roof of my house,
The rainbow returned with me.
To the entrance of my house.
The rainbow returned with me.
To just within my house,
The rainbow returned with me.
To my fireside,
The rainbow returned with me.
To the center of my house,
The rainbow returned with me.

At the fore part of my house with the dawn,
The Talking God sits with me.
The House God sits with me.
Pollen Boy sits with me.
Grasshopper Girl sits with me.
In beauty Estsánatlehi, my mother, for her
    I return.
Beautifully my fire to me is restored.
Beautifully my possessions are to me re-
    stored.
Beautifully my soft goods to me are re-
    stored.
Beautifully my hard goods to me are re-
    stored.
Beautifully my horses to me are restored.
Beautifully my sheep to me are restored.
Beautifully my old men to me are restored.
Beautifully my old women to me are re-
    stored.
Beautifully my young men to me are re-
    stored.
Beautifully my women to me are restored.
Beautifully my children to me are restored.
Beautifully my wife to me is restored.
Beautifully my chiefs to me are restored.
Beautifully my country to me is restored.
Beautifully my fields to me are restored.
Beautifully my house to me is restored.
Talking God sits with me.
House God sits with me.

Pollen Boy sits with me.
Grasshopper Girl sits with me.
Beautifully white corn to me is restored.
Beautifully yellow corn to me is restored.
Beautifully blue corn to me is restored.
Beautifully corn of all kinds to me is re-
    stored.
In beauty may I walk.
All day long may I walk.
Through the returning seasons may I walk.
On the trail marked with pollen may I walk.
With grasshoppers about my feet may I
    walk.
With dew about my feet may I walk.
With beauty may I walk.
With beauty before me, may I walk.
With beauty behind me, may I walk.
With beauty above me, may I walk.
With beauty below me, may I walk.
With beauty all around me, may I walk.
In old age wandering on a trail of beauty,
    lively, may I walk.
In old age wandering on a trail of beauty,
    living again, may I walk.
  It is finished in beauty.
  It is finished in beauty.

NIGHT CHANT
(FOR THE NINTH SONG)

In Tsegihi,
In the house made of dawn,

In the house made of evening twilight,
In the house made of dark cloud,
In the house made of rain and mist, of pol-
    len, of grasshoppers,
Where the dark mist curtains the doorway,
The path to which is on the rainbow,
Where the zig-zag lightning stands high on
    top,
Where the he-rain stands high on top,
Oh, male divinity!
With your moccasins of dark cloud, come to
    us,
With your mind enveloped in dark cloud,
    come to us,
With the dark thunder above you, come to
    us soaring,
With the shapen cloud at your feet, come
    to us soaring.
With the far darkness made of the dark
    cloud over your head, come to us soar-
    ing,
With the far darkness made of the rain and
    the mist over your head, come to us
    soaring,
With the far darkness made of the rain and
    the mist over your head, come to us
    soaring.
With the zig-zag lightning flung out high
    over your head,

With the rainbow hanging high over your
    head, come to us soaring.
With the far darkness made of the dark
    cloud on the ends of your wings,
With the far darkness made of the rain and
    the mist on the ends of your wings,
    come to us soaring,
With the zig-zag lightning, with the rain-
    bow hanging high on the ends of your
    wings, come to us soaring.
With the near darkness made of dark cloud
    of the rain and the mist, come to us,
With the darkness on the earth, come to us.

With these I wish the foam floating on the
    flowing water over the roots of the
    great corn,
I have made your sacrifice,
I have prepared a smoke for you,
My feet restore for me.
My limbs restore, my body restore, my
    mind restore, my voice restore for me.
Today, take out your spell for me,
Today, take away your spell for me.
Away from me you have taken it,
Far off from me it is taken,
Far off you have done it.

Happily I recover,
Happily I become cool,

My eyes regain their power, my head cools,
my limbs regain their strength, I hear
again.
Happily for me the spell is taken off,
Happily I walk; impervious to pain, I walk;
light within, I walk; joyous, I walk.
Abundant dark clouds I desire,
An abundance of vegetation I desire,
An abundance of pollen, abundant dew, I
desire.
Happily may fair white corn, to the ends of
the earth, come with you,
Happily may fair yellow corn, fair blue
corn, fair corn of all kinds, plants of all
kinds, goods of all kinds, jewels of all
kinds, to the ends of the earth, come
with you.
With these before you, happily may they
come with you,
With these behind, below, above, around
you, happily may they come with you,
Thus you accomplish your tasks.

Happily the old men will regard you,
Happily the old women will regard you,
The young men and the young women will
regard you,
The children will regard you,
The chiefs will regard you,
Happily, as they scatter in different direc-
tions, they will regard you,

Happily, as they approach their homes,
they will regard you.

May their roads home be on the trail of
peace,
Happily may they all return.
In beauty I walk,
With beauty before me, I walk,
With beauty behind me, I walk,
With beauty above and about me, I walk,
It is finished in beauty,
It is finished in beauty.

PROTECTION SONG
(TO BE SUNG ON GOING INTO BATTLE)
(*Navajo*)

I

Now, Slayer of the Alien Gods, among men
am I.
Now among the alien gods with weapons of
magic am I.
Rubbed with the summits of the mountains,
Now among the alien gods with weapons of
magic am I.
Now upon the beautiful trail of old age,
Now among the alien gods with weapons of
magic am I.

II

Now, Offspring of the Water, among men
am I.

Now among the alien gods with weapons of
    magic am I.
Rubbed with the water of the summits,
Now among the alien gods with weapons of
    magic am I.
Now upon the beautiful trail of old age,
Now among the alien gods with weapons of
    magic am I.

III

Now, Lightning of the Thunder, among
    men am I.
Now among the alien gods with weapons of
    magic am I.
Rubbed with the summit of the sky,
Now among the alien gods with weapons of
    magic am I.
Now upon the beautiful trail of old age,
Now among the alien gods with weapons of
    magic am I.

IV

Now, Altsodoniglehi, among men am I.
Now among the alien gods with weapons of
    magic am I.
Rubbed with the summits of the earth,
Now among the alien gods with weapons of
    magic am I.
Now upon the beautiful trail of old age,
Now among the alien gods with weapons of
    magic am I.

THE TOWN CRIER CALLS AT DAWN
TO ANNOUNCE THE FEAST
(*Pueblo*)

All people awake, open your eyes, arise,
Become children of light, vigorous, active,
> sprightly.
Hasten clouds from the four world quar-
> ters;
Come snow in plenty, that water may be
> abundant when summer comes;
Come ice, cover the fields, that the planting
> may yield abundance,
Let all hearts be glad!
The knowing ones will assemble in four
> days;
They will encircle the village dancing and
> singing songs . . .
That moisture may come in abundance.

SONG OF THE HORSE

(*Navajo*)

How joyous his neigh!
Lo, the Turquoise Horse of Johano-ai,
> How joyous his neigh,
There on precious hides outspread stand-
> eth he;
> How joyous his neigh,
There on tips of fair fresh flowers feedeth
> he;

How joyous his neigh,
There of mingled waters holy drinketh he;
  How joyous his neigh,
There he spurneth dust of glittering
  grains;
  How joyous his neigh,
There in mist of sacred pollen hidden, all
  hidden he;
  How joyous his neigh,
There his offspring many grow and thrive
  for evermore;
  How joyous his neigh!

SONG OF THE BLUE-CORN DANCE
(Zuñi)

Beautiful, lo, the summer clouds,
Beautiful, lo, the summer clouds!
Blossoming clouds in the sky,
Like unto shimmering flowers,
Blossoming clouds in the sky,
Onward, lo, they come,
Hither, hither bound!

PIMA RITUAL SONG CYCLE
THE FLOOD
ELDER BROTHER, SON OF EARTH
(Chanted by the People)
I

Dazzling power has Elder Brother,
Mastering the winds with song.

Swiftly now we come together,
  Singing to gain control.

II

EARTH DOCTOR PROPHESIED THE FLOOD, CAUSED
    BY ELDER BROTHER:

Weep, my unfortunate people!
  All this you will see take place.
Weep, my unfortunate people!
  For the waters will overwhelm the land.
Weep, my unhappy relatives!
  You will learn all.
Weep, my unfortunate relatives!
  You will learn all.
The waters will overwhelm the mountains.

III

ELDER BROTHER FROM HIS OLLA SONG:

Black house! Black house! Hold me safely
    in;
Black house! Black house! Hold me safely
    in,
  As I journey to and fro, to and fro.

AS HE WAS BORNE ALONG BY THE FLOOD HE
    SANG:

Running water, running water, herein re-
    sounding,
  As on the clouds I am carried to the sky,
Running water, running water, herein roar-
    ing,
  As on the clouds I am carried to the sky.

EMERGING SAFELY FROM THE OLLA HE SANG:

Here I come forth! Here I come forth!
  With magic powers I emerge.
Here I come forth! Here I come forth!
  With magic powers I emerge.
I stand alone! Alone!
  Who will accompany me?
My staff and my crystal
  They shall bide with me.

IV

NOW SOUTH DOCTOR FORETOLD THE DESTRUC-
TION OF EARTH AND ALL ITS CREATURES:

The waters dissolve the land.
  The waters dissolve the land.
The mighty magician tests his strength.
The waters dissolve the mountain.
  The waters dissolve the mountain.
Nasi foresees what is coming.

V

EARTH DOCTOR BEHELD THE RISING WATERS:

Haiya! Haiya! Flood! Flood! Hai-iya!
  See the doom awaiting them!
Haiya! Haiya! Flood! Flood! Hai-iya!
  Here are my doomed people before me.

VI

SOUTH DOCTOR RAISED THE MOUNTAINS:

On the Crooked mountain I am standing,
  Trying to disperse the waters.
On the Crooked mountain I am standing,
  Trying to disperse the waters.

AND MARKED THE LIMITS OF THE FLOOD:
On the Crooked mountain top I'm standing,
    Trying to disperse the waters.
On the Crooked mountain top I'm standing,
    Trying to disperse the waters.

BUT HE COULD DO NO MORE:
Powerless! Powerless!
    Powerless is my magic crystal!
Powerless! Powerless!
    I shall become as stone.

Earth Doctor escaped destruction by shut-
    ting himself in his reed staff.
Elder Brother was saved in the his olla.
    After the waters rolled back
Elder Brother was first to appear and so
    became ruler of the world.
Now Earth Doctor created all things anew.

CREATION SONGS BY EARTH DOCTOR

I

Earth Magician shapes this world.
    Behold what he can do!
Round and smooth he molds it.
    Behold what he can do!

II

Earth Magician makes the mountains.
    Heed what he has to say!
He it is that makes the mesas.
    Heed what he has to say.

Earth Magician shapes this world;
  Earth Magician makes its mountains;
Makes all larger, larger, larger.

III

  Into the earth the Magician glances;
Into its mountains he may see.

IV

I have made the Sun!
  I have made the Sun!
Hurling it high
  In the four directions.
To the East I threw it
  To run its appointed course.

V

I have made the Moon!
  I have made the Moon!
Hurling it high
  In the four directions.
To the East I threw it
  To run its appointed course.

VI

I have made the Stars!
  I have made the Stars!
Above the earth I threw them.
  All things above I've made
'And placed them to illumine.

WARS OF THE PEOPLE
I

AFTER A TIME ELDER BROTHER WENT WITH THE
PEOPLE TO SLAY HÂ-ÂK, THE FEMALE MONSTER

Dazzling power has Elder Brother,
  Mastering the winds with song.
Swiftly now we come together,
  Singing to secure control.
Kovakova, kovakova,
  Kovakova, kovakova.
Singing on the summit
  Of great Mo-hatûk mountain,
Anayokuna, anayokuna, hayokuna.
Sacred pipe of Tcu-unarsat,
  Sleep-inducing sacred pipe,
Anayokuna, anayokuna, hayokuna.
  Hâ-âk flees from her pursuers,
But her spring and mortar stay.
Throw a great stone!
Throw a great stone!
  The blue owl is brightest,
Throw a great stone!
  The blue owl is brightest,
Throw a great stone.

II

WHEN THEY HAD SLAIN HÂ-ÂK THEY WENT
AGAINST THEIR ENEMIES, SINGING:

We go; we go; we go; we go.
  Happy, we leave our homes.

We go; happily we go.
We run; we run; we run; we run.
  Happy, we leave our land.
With pleasure hence we hasten.

III

THUS SANG THE PEOPLE AS THEY CAME UP OUT
  OF THE EARTH, WHITHER THEY FLED DUR-
  ING THE FLOOD:

Together we emerge with our rattles;
Together we emerge with our rattles,
  Bright-hued feathers in our headdresses.

With our nyñnyirsa we went down,
With our nyñnyirsa we went down;
  Wearing Yoku feathers in our head-
    dresses.

This is the White Land, we arrive singing,
  Headdresses waving in the breeze.
We have come! We have come!
  The land trembles with our dancing and
    singing.

      We run, we run, we run, we run,
      Happy we leave our land;
        With pleasure hence we hasten.

On these Black mountains all are singing,
  Headdresses waving, headdresses wav-
    ing.
We all rejoice! We all rejoice!
  Singing, dancing, the mountains trem-
    bling.

IV

Yonder stands the doomed habitation.
  About the pueblo runs its frightened
    chieftain
In yellow garment with hand-print decora-
    tion.

V

AT GILA CROSSING ELDER BROTHER SANG:

I am the magician who with the sacred pipe
  Of Tcu-unarsat increase my magic
    power.
I am the magician of the downy feathers.
  With the soothing sacred pipe
I bring sleep upon my enemy.

VI

THEY WENT AGAINST THE ENEMY NEAR TEMPE,
SINGING:

Look for him! Look for him!
  Poor distracted enemy; take him!
Poor fear-stricken enemy; take him!

VII

WHEN HE CLIMBED THE CLIFF TO ATTACK
EAGLE, ELDER BROTHER SANG:

Up the cliff, steep and smooth,
  Up the cliff, steep and smooth,
Up the cliff, steep and smooth,
  Climbs Elder Brother

With his shining power.
  Up the cliff, steep and smooth,
Up the cliff, steep and smooth,
  He climbs step by step.

VIII

THERE HE CONCEALED HIMSELF AS A FLY,
SINGING:

Himovali! Die fly! Himovali! Die fly!
  I shall sleep! I shall sleep!
Himovali! Let die! I am drowsy.
  I will sleep! Buzz-z.

IX

WHEN EAGLE RETURNED HIS WIFE PUT HIM TO
SLEEP WITH THIS SONG:

Haya yakahai yahai mo! Haya yakahai
  mo!
  I am sleepy, I am sleepy.
Haya yakahai yahai mo! I am sleepy.

X

THEN THE ELDER BROTHER SLEW THE EAGLE AND
RETURNING IN TRIUMPH, ELDER BROTHER
CELEBRATED HIS PROWESS:

Child of the Raven! Child of the Raven!
  You of the dazzling power.
See my magic power shining like the
  mirage.

HUNTING SONGS
I

At the time of the White Dawn;
  At the time of the White Dawn,
I arose and went away.
  At Blue Nightfall I went away.

I ate the thornapple leaves
  And the leaves made me dizzy.
I drank thornapple flowers
  And the drink made me stagger.
The hunter, Bow-remaining,
  He overtook and killed me,
Cut and threw my horns away.
  The hunter, Reed-remaining,
He overtook and killed me,
  Cut and threw my feet away.

Now the flies become crazy
  And they drop with flapping wings.
The drunken butterflies sit
  With opening and shutting wings.

II

Young Hare Magician running
  Brings black-tailed deer venison.
And young Badger Magician
  Brings the feet of black-tailed deer.

Had I neither winds or clouds?
  In the east the Yellow Ikol,
In the west the Yellow Ikol
  Called me. I had no winds or clouds.

BASKET-BEATING SONGS
I

As the Sun sinks to the westward
  We begin singing the Eagle songs.
The home of the Magician rises,
Standing before me in the land.
We begin singing the Eagle songs.

Earth Magician now comes hither;
  Earth Magician now comes hither.
From the depths the songs are rising,
  And by him are here established.
As now the land is prosperous;
  As now the land is prosperous
Elder Brother comes from the East;
  He comes here as a child might,
The land prospers with his coming.

It was in the western mountains
  That White-Eater Woman dwelt.
It was in the western mountains
  That White-Eater Woman dwelt.

The evening glows red in the West,
  And the birds here gather about me.
Now I hear the screams of the Eagle.
  Haiya ha aiya haya haya ha-a!
Now I meet and see you. Haiya ha!
II
Roll from cliff end to cliff end,
  Roll, Winds, from the steep house walls.
Thus the growing excitement

Gathers like the winds that blow
From the house of Wind Magician.

In the East, my younger brothers,
   We are preceded by the bearers
Of the sacred eagle feathers.
   In the East, my younger brothers,
We are preceded by the bearers
   Of the sacred eagle feathers

In the distant land of Eagle,
   In the distant land of Eagle
Sounds the harmonious rolling
   Of reverberating thunder.

Now the Swallow begins his singing;
   Now the Swallow begins his singing.
And the women who are with me,
   The poor women begin to sing.

The Swallows meet in the standing cliffs;
   The Swallows meet in the standing cliffs.
And the rainbows arched above me,
   There the blue rainbow arches meet.

The Black Swallows running hither;
   The Black Swallows running hither,
Running hither come to lead me,
   Lead me there, lead me there.

Haiya! Far in the distant east
   Lie the clouds hidden under the moun-
      tain.

Far in the east direction
　　To the hidden clouds I come running.

We are beating the basket drums:
　　We are beating the basket drums.
I am singing, I am listening;
　　From my feathers clouds are shaking.

I am circling like the Vulture,
　　Staying, flying near the blue.
I am circling like the Vulture,
　　Breathing, flying near the blue.

Now the Reddish Bat rejoices
　　In the songs which we are singing;
He rejoices in the eagle down
　　With which we ornament our headdress.

I ran into the swamp confused;
　　There I heard the Tadpoles singing.
I ran into the swamp confused,
　　Where the bark-clothed Tadpoles sang.

In the West the Dragonfly wanders,
　　Skimming the surface of the pools,
Touching only with his tail. He skims
　　With flapping and rustling wings.

Thence I run as the darkness gathers,
　　Wearing cactus flowers in my hair.

Thence I run as the darkness gathers,
   In fluttering darkness to the singing
     place.

SONG OF THE RACE

Many people have gathered together,
   I am ready to start in the race,
And the Swallow with beating wings
   Cools me in readiness for the word.

Far in the west stands the Black mountain
   Around which our racers ran at noon.
Who is this man running with me,
   The shadow of whose hands I see?

SONG OF STRANGENESS

Singing to the gods in supplication;
   Singing to the gods in supplication,
Thus my magic power is uplifted.
   My power is uplifted as I sing.

Harlots hither running come;
   Harlots hither running come,
Holding blue flowers as they run.
   Talking in whispers they file along.

Along the crooked trail I'm going,
   Along the crooked trail going west.
To the land of rainbows I'm going,
   Swinging my arms as I journey on.

NAME-SONG

The ceremonial reeds are lifted;
　　The ceremonial reeds are lifted.
Ma-akahi has killed an Apache,
　　And we meet together here in war paint
To collect hair trophies with their power.
　　Hivayomi has taken a captive,
And the magic of his bow dies with him.

PUBERTY SONG

Come, hurry forth, hurry forth.
　　Already the echoing sounds
Of darkness are heard around.

The Virgin is not sleepy,
She is wakeful through the night.

The Saguaro lies there broken;
　　And my fallen feathers rise
O'er the top of Table Mountain.

The boy stirred the rumbling stones;
　　The woman heard and could not sleep.
And my toe nails are broken.

The branches of darkness fell,
Cutting my feathers as I passed.

SONG OF THE MAGIC OF DAWN

On the top of Móhatûk
　　There are many clouds standing.
On the top of Móhatûk
　　Many fog clouds are rising.

The bitter wind blows on us;
　The bitter wind blows on us,
As we sing with many bows.

Though I am a Navitco,
　I hear you talk about me.
I thrust my head through the sky
　And with it I run away.

Cut sticks, cut sticks, cut sticks straight.

FETISH SONG

We commence the fetish song;
　We commence the fetish song.
It is difficult but I try;
　The night grows very noisy.

The fetish song arises;
　The fetish song arises.
To it the crazed women run;
　To it the crazed women run.

Pity me!　Oh, pity me!
　And strip away my disease;
Now strip away my disease;
　Clear it away by singing.
I'm going to the singing;
　I'm going to the singing.
It is leading to the mountain,
　Running to Sievat mountain.

LIGHTNING SONG

See the destructive lightning
    Going to kill the distant tree.
It is going, my younger brother,
    To split the distant tree.

Around the mountain I carry
    My poor younger brother:
Carry him around the mountain
    And then stand before it.

The lightning like reddish snakes
    Tries to lash and shiver the trees.
The lightning tries to strike them,
    But it fails and they still stand.

Through the roaring darkness I run,
    Carrying my poor younger brother;
From the top of the sky the lightning
    Shoots, and strikes nearby.

HORNED TOAD SONG

The East Land seems very pleasant.
    I go toward it and I see
How pleasant it seems to be.
    I go toward the Pleasant Land.

West Land is most terrible.
    I go toward it and I see
How terrible the Land is.
    I go toward the fearful Land.

GILA MONSTER SONG

Pitiable harlot though I am,
  My heart glows with the singing
While the evening yet is young.
  My heart glows with the singing.

Where the two stones were standing,
  Black Wind roared in fearful blasts,
Driving the birds before him
  Fluttering back and forth.

On the summit of white Ngiwolik
  There the green frogs are singing.
Lying near the blue storm clouds
  There many frogs are singing.

BLACK LIZARD SONG

We first sing at the Magician's;
  We first sing at the Magician's,
The round disk of the Sun arose,
  Accompanied with its rays.

Harlots came running in a group;
  Harlots came running in a group.
Harlots came with hikimoli,
  Flower crowns upon their heads.

Black Lizard found the trail where
  Elder Brother had been running,
And he came out from the clouds
  With water upon his arms.

Darkness settles on the summit
  Of the great Stony Mountain.
There circling round it settles
  On the great Stony Mountain.

The ruddy beams like spider threads
  Across the sky came streaming.
The reddish snakes like spider's web
  To the opposite side came flaming.

BLACK-TAILED DEER SONG

Down from the houses of magic;
  Down from the houses of magic,
Blow the winds and from my antlers,
  And my ears they stronger gather.

Over there I ran trembling;
  Over there I ran trembling,
For bows and arrows pursued me.
  Many bows were on my trail.

What horse is trying to catch me?
  What horse is trying to catch me?
The horse with the star forehead
  Now slowly gains upon me.

We are sitting here together;
　We are sitting here together,
Singing the song of the east,
　Singing the song of the west.

RATTLESNAKE SONG

In the early evening,
　In the early evening
We begin to sing many songs;
　And I join in singing many.

It was near Kâ-matûk mountain
　That this Rattlesnake came forth;
And he saw the low clouds lying
　Near the summit of the mountain.

Who is this, who is this?
　Is it not Horned Rattlesnake?
Is it not Horned Rattlesnake
　Who now appears before us?

The Butterflies are singing;
　The Butterflies are singing,
As I go past the foundations
　Below, of the ancient house.

BEAVER SONG

You talk about and fear me;
  You talk about and fear me.
As like the sinuous snake
  I go upon the water.

I see that you go slowly;
  I see that you go slowly.
Strong as the Sun among the trees,
  You leave your mark upon them.

Younger brother, I am Beaver,
  I am the quick-eared Beaver
That gnaws the trees of the forest,
  'Tis I who overthrow them.

OWL SONG

Toward great Kâ-matûk mountain
  I go to join the singing,
During the glow of evening.
  I meet all the singers there.

Owl is singing in the distance,
  I hear him moving back and forth.
Many harlots came here running;
  Here came running and came laughing.

Small Owl resembles Tcokot;
  The winds rise from Owl's feathers.

With their ashy tips he starts them.
  Small Owl is like the Large Owl.

Owl makes me drink the reddish water;
  Rapidly intoxicated
I try to walk straight toward the east,
  And find my footsteps staggering.

QUAIL SONG

The Gray quails were bunched together
  Coyote ran to look upon them.
The Blue quails were bunched together;
  Coyote looked sidewise at them.

MOUSE SONG

Wings of birds invisible
  Are now fluttering above you.
You stand with face uplifted
  And quietly listen there.

Our land was unfortunate;
  The floods came rolling westward,
Then they came flowing westward,
  And I cried out much afraid.

BEAR SONG

I am the Black Bear. Around me
  You see the light clouds extending.
I am the Black Bear. Around me
  You see the light dew falling.

I drink the reddish liquor
  Which kills the spirit in me.
I drink the reddish liquor
  Which kills the spirit in me.

Now the singing has commenced,
  Now the singing has commenced.
I go with my younger brother;
  I know the songs we're singing.

ROADRUNNER SONG

Roadrunner with the bushy head
  Is always crying, poi! poi!
As he runs around the house.
  Poi! poi! around the house.

Here is the lonely Roadrunner;
  Here is the lonely Roadrunner.
He eats lizards in the morning;
  He eats solitary lizards.

Here is the red-eyed Roadrunner;
  Here is the red-eyed Roadrunner,
Who runs about the mistletoe.
  This is the red-eyed Roadrunner.

I run and hide! I run and hide!
  Now I kill the Gray Lizard
And I eat his fat body.
  I run and hide! I run and hide.

Over yonder in the mesquite
   Stands the Hawk's nest with its branches
Which rise like kiâhâ frame sticks,
   Over yonder in the mesquite.

DOG SONG

The songs commence at nightfall,
   And the winds blow toward the north.
The winds are blowing strongly,
   Blowing my tail toward the north.

Butterfly wings are falling;
   Butterfly wings are falling,
Falling upon and harming;
   My suffering is greater.

See the small dogs come running;
   See the poor dogs come running.
See the horsemen coming after;
   See the horsemen come laughing.

HARE SONG

Hare is jumping and singing;
   Hare is jumping and singing,
While the wind is roaring.
   While the wind is roaring.

Hare is dancing and singing;
   Hare is dancing and singing,

While the clouds are roaring,
    While the clouds are roaring.

With headdress of owl feathers;
    With headdress of owl feathers,
He comes to my far country;
    He comes bringing hence his bow.

The Gray Mouse came at nightfall;
    The Gray Mouse came at nightfall,
Came running in the darkness;
    Came breathing in the darkness.

I am shut in at day dawn;
    I am shut in at day dawn,
All night I am free to run
    But am shut in at day dawn.

GOPHER SONG

In the reddish glow of nightfall,
    In the reddish glow of nightfall
I return to my burrow,
    About which the flowers bloom.

With the four eagle feathers,
    With the four eagle feathers
I stir the air. When I turn
    My magic power is crossed.

And I make hills of soft earth;
   And I make hills of soft earth.
My breath withers all before it;
   My breath withers all before it.

COYOTE SONG

Coyote commences singing;
   Coyote commences singing.
The young woman hurries forth
   To hear the Coyote songs.

A hat of eagle feathers;
   A hat of eagle feathers,
A headdress was made for me
   That made my heart grow stronger.

Coyote ran around it;
   Coyote ran around it,
Ran into the blue water,
   Changed the color of his hair.

BADGER SONG

Here am I unfortunate;
   Here am I unfortunate,
Not to know the songs to sing;
   The songs we sing at sunset.

There came a Gray Owl at sunset
   There came a Gray Owl at sunset

Hooting softly around me,
   He brought terror to my heart.

The land lay quietly sleeping;
   The land lay quietly sleeping.
My young stretch, crying, haya!
   Pity them digging in the dust.

You Sun out there in the west;
   You Sun out there in the west,
You are now talking to me.
   You are sounding your gourd rattle.

The land is parched and burning,
   The land is parched and burning.
Going and looking about me
   I see a narrow strip of green.

Yet I do not know surely,
   Yet I do not know surely.
The harlot is here among us.
   I go away toward the west.

The shadow of Crooked mountain,
   The curved and pointed shadow.
'Twas there that I heard the singing;
   Heard the songs that harmed my heart.

The light glow of evening;
  The light glow of evening
Comes as the quails fly slowly,
  And it settles on the young.

BUTTERFLY SONG

The Butterfly song we now commence;
  The Butterfly song we now commence,
Dancing on sides to and fro
  Until the dust arises.

The Butterfly Bird, the Butterfly Bird
  Commences to sing his many songs.
I run to where the dust arises,
  Close to the walls of the house.

I commence the song, I commence the song.
  I heard the singing as I ran;
I heard the singing as I ran.
  I join with the singing.

The Cat-tail Woman commences singing;
  The Cat-tail Woman commences singing.
I join the circling dancers,
  Striking my breast and singing.

I sail in the clouds to Table mountain;
  I sail in the clouds to Table mountain,
And I sing with Kâ-matûk mountain
  Upon which there are no clouds.

Hurry to the Dead Standing mountain;
　Hurry to the Dead Standing mountain.
See there, my Younger Brother,
　How the winds there run their course.

At the clearing of Ma-ayal mountain;
　At the clearing of Ma-ayal mountain,
Before the house of the Magician,
　There stands the woman laughing.

Here on the slopes of Crooked mountain;
　Here on the slopes of Crooked mountain,
Around whose crest the foam remains,
　We have run for blue water.

DEMON SONG

Singing at Kâ-matûk mountain;
　Singing at Kâ-matûk mountain,
I listen to their singing;
　I come running to sing with them.

Evening now is falling;
　Evening now is falling,
And demons appeared running
　To strip and expose my soul.

In a Santa Rita cave;
　In a Santa Rita cave,
As I entered in the cave,
　I saw the breath of demons.

Here demon boys came running;
  Here demon boys came running,
Grasping my hair they carried me,
  Brought me to a distant land.

RAIN SONGS

I

Hi-ihiya naiho-o! Let us begin our song,
  Let us begin, rejoicing. Hitciya
    yahina-a.
Let us begin our song, let us begin rejoic-
    ing,
  Singing of the large corn. Hitciya
    yahina-a.
Singing of the small corn. Hitciya
    yahina-a.

II

Hi-ihiya naiho-o! The darkness of evening
  Falls as we sing before the sacred âmina.
About us on all sides corn tassels are wav-
    ing.
  Hitciya yahina! The white light of day
    dawn
Yet finds us singing, while corn tassels are
    waving.
  Hitciya yahina-a! The darkness of eve-
    ning
Falls as we sing before the sacred âmina.
  About us on all sides corn tassels are
    waving.
Hitciya yahina! The white light of day
    dawn

Yet finds us singing, while the squash
    leaves are waving.

Hi-iya naiho-o! The earth is rumbling
    From the beating of our basket drums.
The earth is rumbling from the beating
    Of our basket drums, everywhere hum-
        ming.
Earth is rumbling, everywhere raining.

III

Hi-ihiya naiho-o! Pluck out the feathers
    From the wing of the Eagle and turn
        them
Toward the east where lie the large clouds.
    Hitciya yahina-a! Pluck out the soft
        down
From the breast of the Eagle and turn it
    Toward the west where sail the small
        clouds.
Hitciya yahina! Beneath the abode
    Of the rain gods it is thundering;
Large corn is there. Hitciya yahina!
    Beneath the abode of the rain gods
It is raining; small corn is there.

WAR SONGS
I
Over that black sandy land,
    Over the top came running,
Over the top came running.

The Apache slave was killed
And his hide tanned for leather.

II

Here the warrior, Shining-row,
  Came and saw the night around me.
Young Coyote made a shield house
  And he sat in it shouting,
And that was pleasing to me.
  Young Coyote tied the darkness;
The cigarettes were passed around,
  Four times when he led me there.
The Hawk on Mahyal mountain
  Stood with me beating his wings.

III

There arose in the East Land
  One whom I met there smoking
Flowerlike cigarettes.

Running dazed and falsely speaking
  Pitiable and faint-hearted
I feel at Crooked mountain.

There I'm going, there I'm going.
  I have to drink the liquor
That makes me stagger as I run.

Vulture arose from Sandy hill
  Shining upon the land around.

IV

The Gray Spider magician

He made a square kiâhâ.
He is indeed a magician.

They are shouting, they are shouting,
　　Around the hill of Atci.
The poor people there are shouting
　　As the news of battle comes.

V

Now where is he, where is he,
　　That he has not already come?
Yes, I fear that he has been killed.

You hung the Raven trophies
　　On a pole and danced around them.

Amid the rocks of the mountain
　　The women tried to hide themselves;
But the men ran and killed them.

CORN SONG

Hi-ilo-o ya-a-a! He who sees everything
　　Sees two stalks of corn standing;
He's my younger brother. Hi-ilo-o ya-a-a!
　　He who sees everything, sees the two
　　　　squashes;
He's my younger brother. Hi-ilo-o ya-a-a!
　　On the summit of Ta-atûkah sees the
　　　　corn standing;
He's my younger brother. Hi-ilo-o ya-a-a!
　　On the summit of Ta-atûkah sees the
　　　　squash standing;

He's my younger brother.   Hi-ilo-o woiha!

Hi-ilo-o ya-a-a!   Over Ta-atûkam
  Rise the clouds with their loud thunder-
    ing.
Hi-ilo-o ya-a-a!   Over Ta-atûkam
  Rise the clouds with their loud raining.
Hi-ilo-o ya-a-a!   The Bluebird is holding
  In his talons the clouds that are thun-
    dering.
Hi-ilo-o ya-a-a!   Yellowbird is holding
  In his talons the clouds that are raining.

Hi-ilo-o ya-a-a!   See Elder Brother
  Breathe out the winds that over Ta-atû-
    kam
Drive the clouds with their loud thunder-
    ing.
Hi-ilo-o ya-a-a!   See Elder Brother
  Breathe out the winds that over Ta-atû-
    kam
  The welcome storm clouds are suspend-
    ing.
Hi-ilo-o ya-a-a!   In the great rain clouds
  Let me sing my song of rejoicing.

MAGICIAN SONG
At early dawn I entered,
  Entered in the white light of day.
And my heart flamed with power
  As I entered the magic house.

In the lofty feather house
  His magic is increasing,
And he moves very slowly
  With the power in his heart.

Elder Brother first came forth;
  Elder Brother first came forth,
And with his shining power
  Governed over all the land.

Earth Magician became angry;
  Earth Magician became angry,
And with his magic power
  He destroyed all the houses.

With a Black Snake I tie them;
  With a Black Snake I tie them,
The houses with a Black Snake,
  The houses with a Black Snake.

With a White Snake I tie them;
  With a White Snake I tie them,
The houses with a White Snake,
  The houses with a White Snake.

NAVITCO SONG
The chicken beans are rattling,
  They are rattling as they fall.
The chicken beans are rattling,
  They are rattling as they fall.

And the stone wall arose there,
  And the stone wall arose there.
When the gourd seed was planted
  It made its way through to grow.

WIND SONG

Wind now commences to sing;
  Wind now commences to sing.
The land stretches before me,
  Before me stretches away.

Wind's house now is thundering;
  Wind's house now is thundering.
I go roaring o'er the land,
  The land covered with thunder.

Over the windy mountains;
  Over the windy mountains,
Came the myriad-legged wind;
  The wind came running hither.

The Black Snake Wind came to me;
  The Black Snake Wind came to me,
Came and wrapped itself about,
  Came here running with its song.

Swiftly with a cup of water
  I came running to make you drink.
I make you drink the water
  And turn dizzily around.

Among the white cactus leaves;
   Among the white cactus leaves,
I came running to that place;
   I came running to that place.

SONG OF THE VISION-MAKER

The evening glow yet lingers;
   The evening glow yet lingers,
And I sit with my gourd rattle
   Engaged in the sacred chant.
As I wave the eagle feathers
   We hear the magic sounding.

Puissant Night is shaking me
   Just as he did at the time
When I was taken up in spirit
   To the great Magician's house.

Yellow Bird placed his feathers
   Where they fell on the head of the
      woman;
Making of her a harlot who ran about
   With her hands clasped before her.

Bluebird drifted at the edge of the world,
   Drifted along upon the blue wind.
White Wind went down from his dwelling
   And raised dust upon the earth.

The moonshine abides in me;
   And soon you men and women will see

The reed that I now am blowing
   Bring the Moon down to meet me.

Haiya! The gourd is rattling;
   Haiya! The gourd is rattling.
When I go to see it there
   I surely find it rattling.

It is evening, it is evening.
   And four times at evening
Calls the white-headed Swallow
   As he plucks out his feathers.

Elder Brother cuts his reed,
   Yonder before me now he throws it,
Stepping upon it so that the
   Clouds repeat the sound.

Gray Coyote is a dirty meddler,
   He wears a belt of snake skin.
Gray Coyote is a dirty meddler,
   He wears a belt of snake skin.

Blue Frog-women met and carried me
   To the cloud land in the East.
Blue Frog-women met and carried me
   To where the clouds are standing.

Gray Coyote stood in the forest,
   From his shoulders he plucked feathers
That gave me shining power,
   Plucked wing feathers bearing power.

I entered Yâinupanu mountain
    And saw Elder Brother's land
Marked off with its square corners,
    Marked as in a rectangle.

Yellow Bird carries me to the caves,
    To the distant caves of the mountain,
And we hear the sound of his footsteps
    As he moves upon his way.

Gray Road-runner, the magician,
    As his young cried out with hunger,
Ran about engaged in killing
    Millipeds that he carried home.

The Black Turtle now approaches us,
    Wearing and shaking his belt of night.
The Black Turtle now approaches us,
    Wearing and shaking his belt of night.

The harlot arose and ran about,
    Beating her breast and the air.
The harlot arose and ran about,
    Beating her breast and the air.

Understand, my younger brothers,
    That it is the Sun that gives me
The trance vision that I see.
    The Sun gives magic power.

NOTE

"Tell me," I asked an Indian song-poet who had just taught me a song of his composing, "when you made your song, which came first, words or music?"

The Indian stared at me in puzzled surprise: "I made a song," he answered, "a song *is* words and music—all comes together."

Because Indian poems are therefore really songs, conceived as a very part of the iteration and intonation of music, I have endeavored in my translations to hold in minutest detail to the original rhythm and accent, believing that only thus can the Indian verse sing, through an alien tongue, in its true form.

NATALIE CURTIS.

Santa Fe, New Mexico, September, 1917.

SONG OF THE EARTH

(*Navajo*)

All is beautiful,
All is beautiful,
All is beautiful, indeed.

Now the Mother Earth
And the Father Sky,
　　Meeting, joining one another,
　　Helpmates ever, they.
　　　　All is beautiful,
　　　　All is beautiful,
　　　　All is beautiful, indeed.

Sisnajinni,
Tsodsichl,
> Meeting, joining one another,
> Helpmates ever, they.
>> All is beautiful,
>> All is beautiful,
>> All is beautiful, indeed.

Now Doko-oslid
And Depenitsa,
> Meeting, joining one another,
> Helpmates ever, they.
>> All is beautiful,
>> All is beautiful,
>> All is beautiful, indeed.

And the night of darkness
And the dawn of light,
> Meeting, joining one another,
> Helpmates ever, they.
>> All is beautiful,
>> All is beautiful,
>> All is beautiful, indeed.

Now Hastyeyalli
And Hastyehogan,
> Meeting, joining one another,
> Helpmates ever, they.
>> All is beautiful,
>> All is beautiful,
>> All is beautiful, indeed.

And the white corn
And the yellow corn,
 Meeting, joining one another,
 Helpmates ever, they.
  All is beautiful,
  All is beautiful,
  All is beautiful, indeed.

And the corn-pollen
And the Ripener,
 Meeting, joining one another,
 Helpmates ever, they.
  All is beautiful,
  All is beautiful,
  All is beautiful, indeed.

Life-that-never-passeth,
Happiness-of-all-things,
 Meeting, joining one another,
 Helpmates ever, they.
  All is beautiful,
  All is beautiful,
  All is beautiful, indeed.

  Now all is beautiful,
  All is beautiful,
  All is beautiful, indeed.

HUNTING SONG

(*Navajo*)

Comes the deer to my singing,
Comes the deer to my song,
Comes the deer to my singing.

He, the blackbird, he am I,
Bird beloved of the wild deer,
    Comes the deer to my singing.

From the Mountain Black,
From the summit,
Down the trail, coming, coming now,
    Comes the deer to my singing.

Through the blossoms,
    Through the flowers, coming, coming
        now,
        Comes the deer to my singing.

Through the flower dew-drops,
    Coming, coming now,
    Comes the deer to my singing.

Through the pollen, flower pollen,
    Coming, coming now,
    Comes the deer to my singing.

Starting with his left fore-foot,
Stamping, turns the frightened deer,
    Comes the deer to my singing.

Quarry mine, blessed am I
In the luck of the chase.
    Comes the deer to my singing.

        Comes the deer to my singing,
        Comes the deer to my song,
        Comes the deer to my singing.

SONG OF THE RAIN CHANT
(Navajo)

Far as man can see,
    Comes the rain,
    Comes the rain with me.

From the Rain-Mount,
Rain-Mount far away,
    Comes the rain,
    Comes the rain with me.

O'er the corn,
O'er the corn, tall corn,
    Comes the rain,
    Comes the rain with me.

'Mid the lightnings,
'Mid the lightnings zigzag,

'Mid the lightnings flashing,
    Comes the rain,
    Comes the rain with me.

'Mid the swallows,
'Mid the swallows blue,
Chirping glad together,
    Comes the rain,
    Comes the rain with me.

Through the pollen,
Through the pollen blest,
All in pollen hidden,
    Comes the rain,
    Comes the rain with me.

Far as man can see,
    Comes the rain,
    Comes the rain with me.

SONG FROM THE MOUNTAIN CHANT

(*Navajo*)

Thereof he telleth.

Now of the Holy Youth,
    Thereof he telleth.
Moccasins decked with black,
    Thereof he telleth.

And richly broidered dress,
  Thereof he telleth.

Arm-bands of eagle feathers,
  Thereof he telleth.

And now the rain-plumes,
  Thereof he telleth.

Now of the Male-Rain,
  Thereof he telleth.

Now of the rain-drops fallen,
  Thereof he telleth.

Now of Unending Life,
  Thereof he telleth.

Now of Unchanging Joy,
  Thereof he telleth.

  Thereof he telleth.

CORN-GRINDING SONG
(*Zuñi*)

I

O, my lovely mountain,
  To' yallanne!
O, my lovely mountain,
  To' yallanne!
  To' yallanne!

High up in the sky,
See Rain-makers seated,
Hither come the rain-clouds now,
　　He-ya, ha-ya, he-ya!

Behold, yonder
All will soon be abloom
Where the flowers spring—
Tall shall grow the youthful corn-plants.

II

Lovely!　See the cloud, the cloud appear!
Lovely!　See the rain, the rain draw near!
　　Who spoke?
'Twas the little corn-ear
High on the tip of the stalk
Singing while it looked at me
　　Talking aloft there—
"Ah, perchance the floods
　　Hither moving—
Ah, may the floods come this way!"

III

Yonder, yonder the fair rainbow,
See the rainbow brightly decked and
　　　　painted!
Now the swallow bringeth glad news to
　　　　your corn,

Singing, "Hitherward, hitherward, hither-
     ward, rain,
    "Hither come!
    "Hither come!"
Now hear the corn-plants murmur,
"We are growing, everywhere!
"Hi, yai! The world, how fair!"

KOROSTA KATZINA SONG
(Hopi)

Yellow butterflies,
Over the blossoming virgin corn,
    With pollen-painted faces
Chase one another in brilliant throng.

Blue butterflies,
Over the blossoming virgin beans,
    With pollen-painted faces
Chase one another in brilliant streams.

Over the blossoming corn,
    Over the virgin corn
Wild bees hum!

Over the blossoming beans,
    Over the virgin beans
Wild bees hum!

Over your field of growing corn
    All day shall hang the thunder-cloud;
Over your field of growing corn
    All day shall come the rushing rain.

HE-HEA KATZINA SONG

(*Hopi*)

Corn-blossom maidens
Here in the fields,
Patches of beans in flower,
Fields all abloom,
Water shining after rain,
Blue clouds looming above.

Now behold!
Through bright clusters of flowers
Yellow butterflies
Are chasing at play,
And through the blossoming beans
Blue butterflies
Are chasing at play.

SONGS FROM CALIFORNIA

SONGS OF SPIRITS

I

(*Wintu*)

LIGHTNING

I bear the sucker-torch to the western tree-
ridge.
Behold me! first born and greatest.

II

OLELBIS (THE CREATOR)

I am great above.
I tan the black cloud.

III

HAU (RED FOX)

On the stone ridge east I go.
On the white road I, Hau, crouching go.
I, Hau, whistle on the road of stars.

IV

POLAR STAR

The circuit of earth which you see,
The scattering of stars in the sky which you
see,
All that is the place for my hair.

SONGS OF KUMASTAMXO
(*Yuma*)
I

WHEN THE SPIRIT-WIND APPROACHED

"The Wind is wandering, is wandering;
The Wind is wandering, is wandering."

II

WHEN HE BURNT THE UNCLEAN HOUSE

"The house will burn, will burn.
The house will be crackling, will be crack-
ling.
It will blaze.
We are going to dance.
It is going to be lighted.
It is going to be lighted.
It will blaze.
We are going to dance.
Something bird-like is coming.
Bird-like tracks will be about the place.
We are going to light this unclean house.
It will blaze, blaze."

NOTE.—Where a house had been burnt seeds were
scattered, for the birds to devour.

III

WHEN HE MADE THE RIVER

"This is my water, my water.
This is my river, my river.
We love its water.
We love its foamwood.
It shall flow forever.

It shall flow forever.
When the weather grows hot, it shall rise
  and overflow its banks.
It shall flow forever."

IV

AFTER HE HAD FINISHED HIS CREATING
"Into the earth I go down, go down.
Nothing but earth will I be seeing, will I
  be seeing.
I sink down into the old river-bed,
Down into the interior."

V

WHEN HE RECAME THE EAGLE
"I am springing, springing.
Wing-feathers!
Body-feathers!
On my hands wing-feathers.
On my body body-feathers."

SONGS FROM THE NORTH-
WEST COAST

PRAYERS OF THE TSIMSHIAN
TO NEXNÓX

Nexnóx, Nexnóx!
Chief, Chief!
    have pity upon us!
    else there will be nobody
    to smoke under you!
Nexnóx, have pity upon us!

FOR FAIR WEATHER

Nexnóx, Nexnóx!
Chief, Chief!
    have pity upon us!
Look down and see
    what those under you
    whom you made are doing!
Pull up your foot
    and sweep off your face!
(*"Pull up your foot" means "stop the
rain"; "sweep off your face" means "take
away the clouds."*)

FOR CALM WEATHER

Hold in your breath, Chief,
    that it may be calm.

THREE SONGS FROM THE HAIDA: QUEEN CHARLOTTE'S ISLAND, B. C.

LOVE SONG
Beautiful is she, this woman,
As the mountain flower;
But cold, cold, is she,
Like the snowbank
Behind which it blooms.

THE BEAR'S SONG
*(Whoever can sing this song is admitted
forever to the friendship of the bears)*
I have taken the woman of beauty
For my wife;
I have taken her from her friends.
I hope her kinsmen will not come
And take her away from me.
I will be kind to her.
Berries, berries I will give her from the
    hill
And roots from the ground.
I will do everything to please her.
For her I made this song and for her I
    sing it.

SONG FOR FINE WEATHER
O good Sun,
Look thou down upon us:
Shine, shine on us, O Sun,

Gather up the clouds, wet, black, under thy
　　arms—
That the rains may cease to fall.
Because thy friends are all here on the
　　beach
Ready to go fishing—
Ready for the hunt.
Therefore look kindly on us, O Good Sun!
Give us peace within our tribe
And with all our enemies.
Again, again, we call—
Hear us, hear us, O Good Sun!

BEAR SONG
(*Haida*)

Chief, chief, that I am,
Be careful how you pull your grandfather
　　around.
Be careful how you pull around your grand-
　　father
As you sit beside him.
I am too much of a boy for you.
Chief, chief that I am,

Chief, chief that I am,
I am already far away.
At the cliff, coming from my passage
　　through the mountains,
I hold up my head grandly.
Chief, chief that I am,

I am already far away from it.
From my blue mountain I am now **far**
    away.
On the Island I travel, led about proudly.
From it I am far away.
Chief, chief that I am.

Chief, chief that I am,
They say that I have green mountains.
They say that I went into the creek I **own**
    which stretches its length afar.
Chief, chief that I am.

Chief, chief that I am,
When the sun rises I start traveling **about**.
Now I am lying under a deadfall.
Chief, chief that I am.

Chief, chief that I am,
My power is all taken away,
My power is all taken away.
Chief, chief that I am,
My power is all taken away,
Chief, chief that I am.

Chief, chief, whither did my great **brother**
    wander proudly?
My mind shakes as I go about.
Chief, chief.

Chief, chief,
Tell me where he fell.
I do not know the place.
Chief, chief, chief.

HAIDA CRADLE SONGS
I

Again perhaps you expect to sit up high in
    your father's canoe
  chief-woman, and look around upon all
    things
  in front of Upset-Canoe.
Be careful, be careful, chief-women!

Again perhaps you expect to sit up high in
    your father's canoe,
  chief-woman, and look around the place
  whence abalones come.
Be careful, be careful, chief-woman.

NOTE.—Chiefs' children used to be placed high up on
blankets in the centre of trading canoes so that they
could look about. Here the baby is reminded of what
she used to do in a former existence.

II

Perhaps you are crying and crawling
  to get your grandmother's hand
  which was hurt on a wooden tray with
    square sides, I hear;
  for that you are crying and crawling
  chief-woman, chief-woman,
  crying and crawling.

III

Whence have you fallen, have you fallen?
Whence have you fallen, have you fallen?
Did you fall, fall, fall, fall,
    from the top of a salmonberry bush?

IV

Stop crying, chief's child! Stop crying,
    chief's child!
I do not expect that drums will sound
    again for you, chief's child, if it is for
    that you are crying and wriggling.
Stop crying, great chief's child,
    a child of noble family sits quietly.
Now, now, great chief's child;
    a child of noble family sits quietly.
Stop crying, chief's child! Stop crying,
    chief's child!
I do not expect that they are going to lay
    heavy planks for you again, chief's
    child;
        if it is for that you are crying and
        wriggling.
Stop crying, great chief's child,
    a child of noble family sits quietly.
Now, now, great chief's child;
    a child of noble family sits quietly.

V

One sits here like a common person facing
    the woods.
Say, stop telling lies!

Your mouth will be crooked
    you mosquito-people-trash!
VI

In your father's house, your father's house
    Cape Qóna seagulls eating things
    are making cries.
In the midst of all these things
    you are going to move
    proudly as you sit.
VII

Come, let us take it on our knees!
  Come, let us take it on our knees!
Hand it to one another inside of its father's
    house,
    hand it to one another!
Come, let us take it on our knees!
  Come, let us take it on our knees!
VIII

At that time when my child
    goes about as a youth
    vainly alone
    I shall sit around.
His son
    making a great noise
    went by on the water.
I wonder where he is going!
His son
    making a great noise
    went by on the water.
It must be to the North islands.

IX

Did you make up your mind
    to fall into the cradle
    to fall into the cradle
    to fall in from the top of a spruce-tree?
    to fall in from the top of a salmon-
        berry bush?

X

Be careful, my noble sons!
    you will grow to one another like
    leaves.
Be careful, my own chief!
    Be careful, my own chief!

XI

Are you crying for this, chief?
Are you crying for this, chief?
Are you crying to have your sisters
    put you up higher, chief?
Crying for your cousins to make the people
    as numerous in front of you
    as when people make sea-gulls cry,
    being obliged to step on them,—
For these things are you crying, chief?

XII

You came to me, you came to me, ye he he!
You came to me, you came to me.
You came walking to me, calling me
    "mother,"
    instead of to some one else.
To me my child, who is a chief's child,
    came walking, calling me "mother,"

Mother of noble family,
Mother of noble family, mother of noble
      family,
      mother of noble family, mother of
      noble family.

XIII

Why does he cry softly?
Why does he wriggle as he sits?
He wriggles and cries for grandfather's
      house.

XIV

It is not now as it was in olden times.
Even slaves are beginning to own good
      abalone-shells!

XV

    Dogs, even,
        when they have pups
        to them give their love.
    That is why
        mine I love.

XVI

    Still stands
        Skîlsîs town.
    Do not cry
        upon my knees!

XVII

Why is it
    your slave close by
    (even I, your mother!)

you want something you cannot get,
you say?
You are very foolish,
uncle reborn,
I bore.

XVIII

My child says:
Look around at the waves,—
Then she fools me
with unripe salmon-berries.

XIX

Behind Sea-Lion Town
I was looking around a while;
the future chief I found,
just big enough to walk.
Take care, take care, my own chief!
Take care, my own master!

XX

Women are better than men,
women are better than men.
Women have more property.
Chiefs of my family,
where are you?

XXI

Upon his grandmother's land
my child walks proudly.
For that his foot is dear.
Do not cry!

BILQULA DEATH SONG
He makes me pure
O making pure, making pure!
I destroy not life
I am the life maker.

SONG OF QAQATCGUK
(*Tlingit*)
The man who thought he had perished
    dreams thus about himself:
    I keep feeling
    as if I had gotten home.

SONG OF WOMAN'S PREMONITION
Already I am going,
    I am going to die.
I have dreamed of my son.

SONG OF RAVEN
That Raven must have been a great fellow.
He went down under the sea.
Then they pulled up his nose.
He went through the town for his nose.
When it was given him he started to fly out
    of doors.
He flew out with it.
Why! instead of looking like himself,
    he looks as if he ought to have a drink.
After you have done as he has done
    you can wander about the entire world-
      beach.

CRADLE SONG FOR A GIRL

If I do not take anything to the party
    I shall be ashamed,
    I shall be ashamed.
Little girls, listen.
Little girls, listen.

CRADLE SONG

    Let me shoot a small bird
        for my younger brother.
    Let me spear a small trout
        for my younger sister.

SONG OF LITTLE-LAKE-UP-ABOVE

(*When his people expected others to come
    with food to give them a feast*)
It is before my face every day.
And when I sleep I always think of you.
I long much for you.
Thinking about you comes to me
    like a sudden sickness.

SONG OF SORROW

(*By a woman whose brothers were drowned
    and their bodies not recovered*)
Your reef has beaten me,
    Kágwantan's children.
But take pity on me.
I wonder what I always attend to
    when I wake up in the morning.
Sometime I might see my brothers.

COMPOSED BY SMALL-LAKE-UNDERNEATH

(About a drifting log found full of nails, out of which a house was built. Sung when a feast is about to be given for a dead man)

I always compare you to a drifting log
    with iron nails in it.
Let my brother float in,
    in that way.
Let him float ashore
    on a good sandy beach.
I always compare you, my mother,
    to the sun passing behind the clouds.
That is what makes the world dark.

KAGWANTAN SONG FOR THE FEAST
(When a slave is to be killed)

The words of people
    now snow me under,
    the words of worthless people.

SUNG BY THE WOLF FAMILIES
(Coming to a feast)

A rich man is coming.
Your feelings you keep silent.
When it is ended,
    thus they always say:
    "It is all gone."

AT A GREAT FEAST
We are also going to be invited
    to Killisnoo.
High-cast people
    are going to eat.

BY NAQUALI
I wonder what my future life
    will do to me.

SONG OF FOR-A-TOWN SPIRIT
*(About the Táqdentan, because when the
    latter came to Juneau to drink they did
    not pay any attention to the Auk
    people.)*
I observe how people are treated
    after they are dead,
    and therefore I drink
    before I die.
What you did was very selfish,
    Táqdentan's children.
But I do not blame you
    for your words.
It is this Raven's fault.

BY NIGOT
What do you think I live for?
I live to drink whiskey.
Have pity on me,
    foam children.

BY TSAKAK
It is only crying about myself
 that comes to me in song.

BY ONE OF THE LENEDI
(*About Juneau when gold was first found
there*)
 Do not talk any more,
  Lenédi's children.
 You are ahead
  of all the people in the world.

AN ANGRY SONG COMPOSED BY SEXDAGWET
(*Against Little Raven, a blind man of
Tongas*)
Just as if a man chased him
 out on the beach
 because of some one's talking,
 Little Raven threw himself
 before my words.
I do not feel even a little numb.
That fellow, Little Raven,
 whose words
 they are always reporting to me,
 can not see anything.

   (*On the same subject*)
Little Raven,
 I hate what you keep saying,

because you are a slave's son
and can see nothing.
I hate to have you talk to me
because you have spots all over your
face
like a big sea cucumber
and look like a slave.
Don't you know that,
because you can not see anything,
you big slave's son,
you keep picking up sand
instead of dipping into the dish?

BY DEAD-SLAVE

(*About a woman named Poor-orphan, who
was a very poor girl, but afterward
became the richest woman in Wran-
gell*)
I used to make fun
of this poor little girl at Wrangell
when she was very small.

BY A SHAMAN OF THE KAGWANTAN
NAMED KAGANK

It is only on account of Strong Drink
that you pity me.
Why don't you also love me?

BY UNDER-A-BLANKET

(*About the son of Luknaxádi, whose
brother was killed in compensation for
the killing of her brother*)

His mind is just like mine,
    Lubnaxádi's children.
So that I am beginning to love him.
I wonder what I always look for
    when I wake up in the morning.
Sometime I might see my brothers.

BY MAN-THAT-IS-NOT-ALL-RIGHT

(*About Princess Thom*)
Even from a house of Strong Drink
    men get away,
    but not from you,
    Raven woman.

BY AMONG-THE-BRANT

(*When his wife had been taken from him*)
Like one who desires Strong Drink,
    I never sleep,
    Toqyédi's children.

(*On the same subject*)
My own mind is very hard to me.
It is just as if
    I were carrying my mind around.
What is the matter with you?

BY OTHER-WATER
(Over a dead man)

My younger brother has brought me
    great joy of laughter.
If I knew the way they go,
    I would go right to him.

BY JOINED-TOGETHER
(When all his friends went down the rapids at Gonaxó and were drowned)

I always look expectantly
    to see some one
    stand up in front of the town
    and in the bay.
I always compare my brothers
    to the people the duck tribe saved.
They went right down under the earth
    like those high-cast people.

BY HERE-IS-A-FEATHER
(When his brother died)

It is as if my grandfather's house
    were turning over with me.
Where is the person who will save me?

BY MAN-FOR-HIMSELF

I love you from my heart,
    Tsaguédi's children.
You are the only one
    I will die with.

BY CGWATC
(About an uncle who had died)
I always think within myself
that there is no place
where people do not die.

MOURNING SONG OF SAKWET
(About her brother who was drowned)

I am like the people
who were killed
by the south wind.

(On the same subject)
Perhaps my brother went
into the sun's trail
so that I can never see him again.

PEACE-SONG AFTER A GREAT WAR
If you had died,
　　Kágwantan's children,
　　I would have cut off my hair for you
I love you so much
　　I would have blackened my face for
　　you,
　　Kágwantan's children.

SONG OF A HUMMING-BIRD DEER
I am feeling very lonely away.
I am going to my uncle's town.
I am singing inside, my masters.
I am crying about myself.

BY LQENA

*(When he was the only one of his people
saved and his enemies wanted to make
peace with him. He danced as a deer,
singing this song and at the end of it
cut in two the man standing next to
him)*

I did this way regarding myself.
I would not let what my conscience
    said to me, pass.
Before his death I saw his ghost.
At once he stabbed
    and killed Cadasíktc.

BY QAUCTE

(Who married a Téqoedi woman)

After you have been drinking
    you had better stop talking
    about how well you were brought up,
    Téqoedi's children.
What one of you thinks about it,
    when he is sober?

LOVE SONG OF A TAGISH WOMAN

    Why have I come to you
        to Dyea from far inland
        only to find
        that you have gone away?
    Here I am,
        crying for you.

LOVE-SONG OF SIQUET, THE DANCER

I wonder what this coming July morning
    will be like.
My mind is very weak
    thinking that I shall be unable
    to see my sweetheart.

BY RAVEN-SKIN
(When his sweetheart abandoned him)

If one had control of death
    it would be very easy
      to die with a Wolf woman.
It would be very pleasant.

MOURNING-SONG OF THE KAGWAN-TAN

It is his own fault
    that this man of the Wolf people died.
Do not lay the blame on any one else.

SPELL SONG
(Kwakiutl)

What of olden times,
    shall I tell you of olden times
    what of olden times
    my grandchildren?
You of olden times,
    you of olden times,
    a cloud,
    lay on the mountains.

CHINOOK SONGS

Songs of the Man
I
Ya, that is good!
Ya, that is good!
That worthless woman
    does not like me.
II
Very unhappy I was
    with my wife,
    in Victoria.
Nobody
    said good-day to us
    in Victoria.
III
Aya, aya!
    I have seen
    Sitka your country.
Never mind, if I die
    now soon.

SONGS OF THE WOMAN
I
I don't care
    if you desert me.
Many pretty boys are in the town.
Soon I shall take another one.
That is not hard for me!

II

Nothing shall bother my mind now.
Don't speak to me. I wish I were dead
    with my sister.

III

Ya ya,
When you take a wife,
Ya ya,
Don't become angry with me.
I do not care.

IV

I am very glad
    when the steamboat comes here.
I think I shall cry
    when the steamboat leaves.

V

I broke down! my dear!
Say good-bye!
    to me now.
Always I cry
    for I live far away.

SONGS FROM THE
FAR NORTH

SONGS FOR THE GREAT FEAST TO THE DEAD

I

For our children are gone,
  While those of our friends remain.
      Ai-ya-ya-yai.
Come back, nephew, come back, we miss
      you;
      Ai-ya-ya-yai.
Come back to us, our lost ones,
  We have presents for you.
      Ai-ya-ya-yai.
Oh, my brother, come back to me,
      Ai-ya-ya-yai.
Come back, my brother, I am lonely,
      Ai-ya-ya-yai.
My brother come back and we
  Will give you a small present,
      Ai-ya-ya-yai-yae-yai, etc.

My children, where are you?
      Ai-ya-ya-yai.
Come back to us, our children,
  We are lonely and sad.
      Ai-ya-ya-yai.

II

Come, my brother,
Return to us again;
We wait for you;
Come, brother, come.

Ai-ya-ya-yai.

Return once more.
Our mother, come back to us.

Ai-ya-ya-yai.

Return, our father;
We wait for you;
Come back to us,
And we, who are lonely,
Will give you food.

Ai-ya-ya-yai.

III

Dead ones, come here;

A-la'-ai-ya'

Come here, do.
  sealskins for a tent you will get.

A-la'-ai-ya'

Come here, do.
    reindeer skins for a bed you will get,

A-la'-ai-ya'

IV

We will sing a song.
We will go down the current.
The waves will rise;
The waves will fall.
The dogs will growl at us.

ESKIMO SONGS

OXAITOQ'S SONG

I walk so long thus
    inland, inland.
I walk so long thus
    inland, inland, and inland.
I am not loved
    inland, inland.
I am not loved
    she is the greatest of all
    inland and inland.
They love best
    inland, inland.
They love best
    what I obtain
    inland and inland.
They love best
    inland, inland.
They love best
    the food that I bring
    inland and inland.

SUMMER SONG

Ajaja, it is pleasant,
    it is pleasant at last
    the great world
    when it is summer at last.

Ajaja, it is pleasant,
    it is pleasant at last
    the great world
    when our caribous begin to come.
Ajaja, they make great noise,
    they make great noise,
    the brooks there in our country
    when it is summer.
Ajaja, this great water
    has spread over the ice;
    I cannot walk
    to the rock across there.
Ajaja, I feel sorry for them,
    I feel sorry for them,
    not being able to speak,
    these gulls.
Ajaja, I feel sorry for them,
    I feel sorry for them,
    not being able to speak,
    these ravens.
A great animal comes now;
    no one observes it;
    I keep it secret;
    the ravens do not tell.

Food like that I cannot obtain.
    but quickly I got
    little sculpins.
Ajaja, he has found a smooth slope,
    he has found a smooth slope,

to burrow into,
the bad old fox.

SEDNOR AND THE FULMAR
(*recitative*)

An Eskimo Ballad

Where is she
    who would never marry?
In a kayok to the mainland
    going away.
Dost thou see, my eyes,
    dost thou see them?
Ia, ha, ha, ha, ha!
To a tent of ragged skins,
    he has brought her, crying;
      (*the Fulmar, her husband*)
Her father with her elder brother
    in a boat coming;
      (*he, seeking his daughter*)
In a boat his daughter embarked.
Her husband, the Fulmar, cried:
      (*thus the Magician!*)
The Fulmar says: "My means for trans-
    forming
    let me see them as they are;
    let me see them once more."

Now they are taking the woman back;
 to the tent going home;
 the Fulmar followed,
 (*thus the Magician!*)
Wind very strong to come near them;
 (*he made, the Magician!*)
 they were shipwrecked, nearly.
 (*Her father fears death!*)
His daughter he pushes
 into the sea.
To the boat on both sides—
 to the boat she clings.
 (*Still followed, the Fulmar!*)
With a knife he struck her;
 whales emerged.
Again he struck her;
 a thong seal emerged.
Again he struck her;
 a fiord seal emerged.
 (*thus the Magician!*)
Her whole body she leaned.
 (*Sednor, fearing death!*)
With a knife into the eyes
 he stabbed her;
He killed her.
 (*Thus the Fulmar, the Magician!*)
On the shore
 her father lifted her.
A quilt he took;
 on the beach laid her down.

With a dog skin she was covered,
    (*Sednor, the Beautiful!*)
The flood-tide took her.

(*Based on a literal translation.*)

INTERPRETATIONS

SUMMER DAWN
(*Tem-Eyos-Kyi*)

She comes—Tem-Eyos-Kwi—
The maiden who has known love!
Last night Love touched her in the house
    of waiting.
Love hid the seeds of life in her garments.
In the wind of her walking they are scat-
    tered;
All the sod will bloom with them!
None shall be lost: because of her glad-
    ness, the gladness of love known.

Ah—hi-i! She sees the earth not as we see
    it—
We who were not overtaken by Love in the
    house of waiting.

Wake, women, maidens and wives!
Greet Tem-Eyos-Kwi!
Greet her with feet dancing,
With songs of the heart and lips trembling
    to silence,
Hands that lift their wonder to the breast
Yet touch not the flesh.

Wake, sons, lovers, young chiefs, hunters
with arrows!

Sharpen the darts, make strong, bend the
bow;

Keen, keen as light, and clear as the wind
be your eyes!

The women await you in secret places,

They have hidden themselves in the leafy
shelters :

All the green leagues of the forest are
ashake with invitation.

The quick beating of their hearts is the
whisper along the bending grass.

The sod grows warm—O men, Summer-
dawn is the spirit of the women!

They have washed their hearts with
prayer,

And their bodies with juices of cedar:

Perfumed and dried by the wind they have
came up from the shore—

The great hosts of the women—

Unwrapping themselves from the mists of
the morning.

They have entered the forest with the foot-
falls of muted music,

With light tossing steps like the spray on
long beaches.

The swinging trees drip dew:

With lines of sparkling rain they point the
    way the women have gone,
Leaving all the paths to them open.

*Harken! They follow Tem-Eyos-Kwi,
    singing:*

  "Come, come, O swift and strong!
We are the women: seek us!
Our hearts, like little swallows, nest above
    the secret pools.
Oh, say, shall not the winged dart pierce,
And the shadow of the bended bow
Stir the still, deep pools?
Oh, the waters shall sparkle and leap and
    mingle,
And brim at your lips, O men!
They shall be poured out and drip upon a
    chief's feet;
They shall fill the hollows of his house with
    children!
Flowing in laughter and whispers and
    little cries
As smoke through the smoke-hole at eve-
    ning!
Ai! ah! ai! Women! Waken the soil with
    freshets;
Bear joy upward as a canoe with sails,
    swifter than paddles.
O men, hunters of life,

We are the harborers, the fosterers—the
    women:
Seek us!''
It was the women, the harborers, the fos-
    terers, who rose first,
And followed Tem-Eyos-Kwi:
They called to the men.

   The men go forth like one!
Lightning and heat are their weapons,
    hurled crashing before them.
Their hairs, spreading wide, give black
    wings to the sun,
As a cloud filled with eagles blown up from
    the sea.
They enter the forest with the tramp of
    thunder and the darkness of storm;
And the song of the women is stilled.
The cry of offering ascends, it passes the
    swooping shadows;
There is a sigh through the forest of winds
    sinking—
Then the hush.

   On the leaves is a sweet whisper of rain,
Whispered sweetness of pangs past.
The warm soil drinks the coolness of
    tears—
Tears that are dropping melodies

Because cunning hands and strong have
  shaken the living cords.
The skies part, the black wings fold;
The Sun-chief's canoe rides on the upper
  blue with furled sails:
Tem-Eyos-Kwi, laughing, is at the paddle.
Our village is drenched with light.
(Ei-i! Tem-Eyos-Kwi is glad because Love
  has overtaken us;
Because now we see the earth as she sees
  it.)
Two by two, they come up from the forest
  —the men and the women.
The women's smiles are the little sun-
  tipped clouds
Floating across the face of the mountain:
The look in their eyes is deeper than seas.
High in the light the men lift their heads.
On their clear brows is the mystic mark
Of those from whom a great dream has
  gone forth.
Firmly they hold the hands of the women,
Who have given peace to their strength,
  and a meaning.
Together, together, the race-makers enter
  the lodges.

SONG OF THE SEARCH

I descend through the forest alone.
Rose-flushed are the willows, stark and
  a-quiver,

In the warm sudden grasp of Spring;
Like a woman when her lover has sudden-
    ly, swiftly taken her.
I hear the secret rustle of the little leaves,
Waiting to be born.
The air is a wind of love
From the wings of eagles mating—
O eagles, my sky is dark with your wings!
The hills and the waters pity me,
The pine-trees reproach me.
The little moss whispers under my feet,
"Son of Earth, Brother,
Why comest thou hither alone?"

    Oh, the wolf has his mate on the moun-
    tain—
Where art thou, Spring-daughter?
I tremble with love as the reeds by the
    river,
I burn as the dusk in the red-tented west,
I call thee aloud as the deer calls the doe,
I await thee as hills wait the morning,
I desire thee as eagles the storm;
I yearn to thy breast as night to the sea,
I claim thee as the silence claims the stars.
O Earth, Earth, great Earth,
Mate of God and mother of me,
Say, where is she, the Bearer of Morning,
My Bringer of Song?
Love in me waits to be born,
Where is She, the woman?

SONG OF WHIP-PLAITING

In the dawn I gathered cedar-boughs
For the plaiting of thy whip.
They were wet with sweet drops;
They still thought of the night.
  All alone I shredded cedar-boughs,
Green boughs in the pale light,
Where the morning meets the sea,
And the great mountain stops.
  Earth was very still.

I heard no sound but the whisper of my
    knife,
My black flint knife.
It whispered among the white strands of
    the cedar,
Whispered in parting the sweet cords for
    thy whip.
O sweet-smelling juice of cedar—
Life-ooze of love!
My knife drips:
Its whisper is the only sound in all the
    world!

Finer than young sea-lions' hairs
Are my cedar-strands:
They are fine as little roots deep down.
(O little roots of cedar
Far, far under the bosom of Tsa-Kumts!—

They have plaited her through with love.)
Now, into my love-gift
Closely, strongly, I will weave them—
Little strands of pain!
Since I saw thee
Standing with thy torch in my doorway,
Their little roots are deep in me.

In the dawn I gathered cedar-boughs:
Sweet, sweet was their odor,
They were wet with tears.
The sweetness will not leave my hands,
No, not in salt sea-washings:
Tears will not wash away sweetness.
I shall have sweet hands for thy service.

(Ah—sometimes—thou wilt be gentle?
Little roots of pain are deep, deep in me
Since I saw thee standing in my doorway.)

I have quenched thy torch—
I have plaited thy whip.
I am thy Woman!

SONG OF THE YOUNG MOTHER

M'-m'-m'-m'-n!   N'-n'-n'-n'-m!
Ai-i-he-i—ah-o-he-a-i-ne—
Swing my chiefling fragrantly
On the cedar-branch.

Cedar, Cedar, tenderly
Sway to the singing wind.
Bright flying Wind with song in thy white
    throat,
And light in thy wide sea-eyes,
The sky's blue feathers on thy wing—
Oh blow, blow, gently, softly, Wind,
Rock my chiefling, Wind,
In his little woven cradle.
In the dusk my fingers still threaded,
Needing no light.
I remember my mother sat near me often,
    watching;
Sometimes weeping. Yes, she wept;
Yet answered not when I asked wherefor.
In the night thou hast waked me at his
    side—
Dancing, in thy dark house, to the doors
    that soon must open
On thy white shining dawn-shores of life:
And I have seen the Moon-Woman's round
    face
Laughing through the smoke-hole, mock-
    ing,
Pointing to thy empty cradle hanging.
Ai! but her smile grew kind! She said,
"Wait a little longer, impatient one;
When next my round face peeps through
    the smoke-hole,
I will seek him at your breast."

Ai-i-hi! Very precious is the man-child!
Ere it is born a woman loves it.
How cam'st thou here, little Chiefling?
A woman gave thee life!

   Yes — my mother wept, watching **me**
     weave for thee . . .
And I have wept, too, a little.

   Strange, that pain came with love;
I knew it not until thy father sought me.
Yet—what woman would cast love out?

   Gladly in the dusk I waited him—
None told me, not my mother even, of the
     pang.
So my heart, joyous, sounded a song of
     drums,
Beating the loud wild march for his swift-
     trampling feet.
The breasts of love were as the eaves of
     a house,
Jutting through the red mists and the dusk
     of ending day,
Calling the hunter to enter to his rest.
The door trembled with strange winds—
He circled my house with the arms of
     strength,
And took me with weapons . . . Joy?
Ay. Yet I cried from the depths with **a**
     sudden deep cry,

And in grieving earth was the torch
   quenched.
. . . Darkness . . . and his, his utterly, in
   that dark . . .
None had told me . . .
Nor that his strength would leap, rejoicing
   at my cry.

   At dawn—it is our custom—I went forth
      alone
Into the mists that wrap the sleeping cedars
And droop to the pale unwakened sea.
Alone on the dawn's white rim I gathered
   cedar-boughs.
My tears fell, shining among the earth's
   bright drops;
For now I knew
Why the maiden plaits a whip of cedar-
   fibre,
To give into her husband's hand on her
   marriage-day.
Once I asked my father—it seemed so
   strange
A maid should weave and weave a rod for
   her own sorrow.
He laughed and said: "It is our custom;
   ay, an old custom—
I know not if it means aught now,
Or ever did have meaning."
My mother sat near. Ay, I have remem-
   bered that she spoke not;

But, silently, in the shadow of his body,
  drooped her head.

  Ay, 'tis old, the custom,
Old as earth is old;
Ancient as passion,
Pitiless as passion—
Ay, pitiless, pitiless, the earth-way for
  women!
Bitter it is, as the taste of bright sea-water,
That he, who takes the gift, and wields our
  weaving of desire,
Knows not the meaning of the gift—nor
  can know ever!
Into the heedless hand of passion
We yield our power-of-pain . . .

It is the law of the earth-way.

  So it is with birth-giving.
Aii-he! the mightier pang,
The mightier loving!
And thou and thy father, the two **Strong**
  Ones,
Glad, glad of the woman's pain-cry!

  M'-m'-m'-m'-n—Ai-i-he-i—
Sleepest thou, little Fatling?
Ay, thou didst long drink at my **breast—**
(But hast not drained it of love.)
Cedar, Cedar, carefully
Guard my little brown cone

On thy earth-bending branch.
M'-m'-m'-m'-n—Ai-i-he-i—
Little life-bud on the bough!
Sleep, sleep, thou drowsy one—
Thou art guarded well.
Ay, rock, rock, safely, safely, little **Man-**
     Child—
A woman watches thee.

SONG OF BASKET-WEAVING

Kulasgh, Kulasgh, my mother,
I sit at thy knee
Weaving my basket of grasses,
Weaving for my harvest of berries when
     the Ripe Days come.
Thy fingers gently touch my hair with fra-
     grance,
Thy mouth drips a song, for the wind has
     kissed it—
(Love sings in thy mouth!)
The soil listens and answers;
I feel a stirring beneath me and hear buds
     opening,
The river chants thy song and the clouds
     dance to it.
Tonight the stars will float upon thy sing-
     ing breath,
Gleaming like slanting flocks above the sea.
All the earth sings: and its voices are one
     song!

I alone am silent: I alone, a maid waiting
    him, the Fate,
The Stirring One, the Planter of the Har-
    vest,
The Basket-Filler.
Kulasgh, Kulasgh, Mother!
See how beautiful, how liberal, is my
    basket,
How tightly woven for the waters of Love,
How soft for the treading of children's
    feet,
How strong to bear them up!
Kulasgh, Kulasgh, Mother, remember me—
Ere the Sunset and the Dropping Leaf!

NOTE.—Kulasgh, Cedar tree, considered the source of
life by the British Columbian Coast tribes, as it sup-
plies all their necessities, even food in fish famine.

THE CHANGE-SONG

  Death's first snows are drifting on my
    cheek,
Pale are my lips
As the kiss of Cin-Uza;
I lie low and still.
Near me crouch my silent kinsmen,
They hold the breath and wait the hour of
    wailing;
They have wrapped the scarlet mourning
    blanket
Round the shoulders of the oldest man;
He has taken their sorrow.

He droops at my door
Like a bleeding hawk where the eagles have
    battled.
He is so old he feels not any grief,
His heart is cold,
In his ears no sound is,
And in his eyes no light.
Therefore have my kinsmen given him
    their griefs—
Because the dawn leaps clear into their
    eyes,
Because the sound of women's feet
Rustling on the cedar mats when the torch
    is blown
Calls sweetly to their ears,
And their hearts are beating for the hunt.
They may not bear the sorrow of my pass-
    ing,
We have known strong joys together!

   I take your loves, my kinsmen,
I leave with you no griefs!
Sing, my kinsmen, when ye swing me
To the topmost branches of the cedar.
Sweet-smelling arms of cedar, reach for
    me,
Tenderly receive me,
Hold me in the Last Caress under open
    sky!
Sing, my kinsmen, when the oldest man

Takes his lone trail through the forest.
He will wear no mourning-blanket when
    he comes again tomorrow!
He will say, "Rejoice—
I have borne your grief afar,
I have buried it deep,
The place is not known."
The wind of your singing shall rock me
In the arms of my mother, the cedar.
Yet there is a sweeter song, my kinsmen;
It is the Change-Song of Supreme One.
I hear it now,
He chants it to my heart;
Because pale death has crossed my thres-
    hold, and has clasped my hand.
"Fear not," sings Supreme One;
"I am making pure, making pure,
I destroy not life,
I am Life-maker!"

    The oldest man has entered the forest.
Ah! Ah! my kinsmen are wailing;
They saw me depart with Death
Into the White Change.
But I go on—and on!
And I sing the Change-Song of Supreme
    One:
Ha- eohos la no-ya ai-a me la-la
Q' oalahag' i-h-e-e la-wo!

SONG OF THE FULL CATCH

Here's good wind, here's sweet wind,
Here's good wind and my woman calls me!
Straight she stands there by the pine-tree,
Faithful waits she by the cedar,
She will smile and reach her hands
When she sees my thousand salmon!
Here's good wind and my woman calls me.

Here's clear water, here's swift water,
Here's bright water and my woman waits
    me!
She will call me from the sea's mouth—
Sweet her pine-bed when the morning
Lights my canoe and the river ends!
Here's good wind, here's swift water,
Strong as love when my woman calls me!

SPRING TO THE EARTH-WITCH

Pai-iya to Swi-ya Kwenewesals

My eyes I will not cover!
I am Pai-iya, stepping free on the goat-
    hills behind thy village.
Blue shadows and white mists, like flowers,
Lie deep in thy green forests.
Night lingers in thy hair;
Pools of starred dusk are thine eyes.
Thy speech is gray fog, impenetrable,
Shrouding the port of the crimson lure—
(The ships of the trusting one are broken).

Oh, flower-red is thy girdle at morning **and**
    evening!
If it were loosened there would be **a race**
    of men,
And thou the harbor of a thousand **won-**
    dering ships.
I have lifted dawn before me as a shield,
Swi-ya Kwen-e-we-sals!

    The Raven pecks beside thy door;
On thy roof the Thunder-Bird claps **his**
    wings;
Thy smile darkles across the skies.
Thy smile is death—
My heart is the riven sea beneath.
If thy scarlet girdle were unknotted **would**
    it stem the sea of my wound?
Nay! Call not me with the wind blow-
    ing through thy garments!
I have bound the mountains to my feet,
Swi-ya Kwen-e-we-sals!

    Last night I saw winged stars in flight
Circling o'er thy dwelling.
They swung at rest on the points of **the**
    shore pine—
Torches red-spanning the bay.
My wolves, at my call,
In long gray troops fled up from the **for-**
    est.

They sphered in guard about me—sleep-
    ing on my shield poised on the four
    world-crags—
As darkened silver cloud-mists wind about
    the moon.
I have shepherded them into the canyon
    between us—
(But my eyes I will not cover!)
Wilt thou come, daring, among my fanged
    flocks,
Swi-ya Kwen-e-we-sals?

    What is this warmth stealing to my
      height
Like footsteps of a strange desire?
Wave on wave of pink and gold breaks
    over the white;
The petals open, chirring,
As if they were feathers on the Song-bird's
    swelling throat.
My wolves, with heads hanging and fangs
    covered, slowly moving, moving,
Huddle in the valley like sky-shadows be-
    fore rain.
Whose steps flow and ripple over the dark
    moss,
Parting the green walls of cedars,
Blossoming among my mating flocks?
Whence this unraveling of flame blown
    loose across the air?

My eyes I will not cover!
I have woven thongs of the mountain mists
And bound me to the morning star.
Between the cliffs of Night and Day, thou
     emergest!—
Thy sod-brown bosom, the mystical craving
     eyes above;
The yearning fragrance of thy closed
     hands,
The wild winds between thy feet,
And the rivers under thy girdle!
I have cast down the great shield of the
     dawn!
Come, redden its rim with me,
Swi-ya Kwen-e-we-sals!

CHIEF CAPILANO GREETS HIS NAMESAKE AT DAWN

White Head of Waters, White Head of
     Light—
Capilano; Cla'h'ya.
White head of the Chief to thee lifts greet-
     ing.
I am hoar with years as thou, great Fa-
     ther;
My hair hangs like the dropping ice
Of thy highest hushed waters.
I have lived a hundred years at thy foot,
Singing the prayer of thanks for life:

"O Kia-Kunaë, Great Spirit One, Great
Kind One,
I praise thee for life, I serve thee with
living,
I bless thee that in kindness thou hast made
the earth
And with love covered it.
Yea, by thy kindness, men and trees stand
forth;
Silently, to me, speak they the speech of
brothers.
For delights the little rivers come among
the hills,
Shining with the smiles of women;
Ay, as the merry murmuring of many
maidens
Are the rivers; swift and tender in their
coming.
(Because thou art kind, Kunaë, thou
madest women.)
It is the morn, Kunaë, I pray, I praise
thee."
Ah!—how many hundred years hast thou
prayed thus, Capilano?
With thee this day, Mountain-Father, I
thank Kunaë for another dawn.
I am girt with blanket and rope of cedar-
fibre;
In my ear is a ring of fine bark.

Thou art belted with innumerable pine-
 trees;
To thee they are smaller than feathers.
The sun is the cedar-ring in thine ear,
The long sea asleep is the spear in thy
 hand.
It is still, with pale lights on the distant
 blade,
Pointing at rest to islands beyond the drop-
 ping sky.
Thou art come forth, as a hunter, to the
 dawn,
Herding the antlered shadows down the
 forest slope.
Their swift fleeing hoofs strike fire from
 the beaten sandshores of morning,
And the black wraiths swoon upon the
 bright opening sea.
With blood of his proud throat crimsoning
 the eastern sky
The great Stag of the Dark in the van falls
 dying.

. . . . . .

Here was I chief ere the coming of the
 white man;
Now is his village spread from this sea
 beyond my sight.
His canoes are floating villages;
They go by with a great noise and a black
 smoke.

His deeds are mighty; they leap with roar-
ing clouds and thunder-fires
Into the blue quiet morning and the white
moon-sky.

.   .   .   .   .   .

Yet have I heard no sound mightier
Than the sun shattering the night
On thy stone shoulder, Capilano.
Yet have I seen no sight more wonderful
and fair
Than the coming of the light,
When Day, the silver-winged gull, down-
swooping finds the sea.
Yet have I known no thing sweeter,
stronger,
Than the smell of piney winds and blue
rippling sea-water,
And the kindness of Kunaë-Kia, the living
One,
Waking the heart of the old chief
To another dawn of life.

THE WILD WOMAN'S LULLABY

What shall I sing to thee, Babe on my back?
Song of the Eagle that mates with the
storm!
Hi-i-ri-i-ki! Ri-eek!
The wild gale is weeping, driven before him
To his nest on the black lone mast of the
night;

Swinging, swinging, far out, high out, over
    the sea!
Hi-i-ri-i-ki! Ri-eek!
Thy father is Eagle-Go-High, chief of thy
    tribe:
Fiercest in war, wisest in council, swiftest
    in hunting,
Harshest and fondest in the tent of his
    woman;
He is my mate!

What shall I sing to thee, Babe on my back?
Song of the wind that is wanton forever!
Fleeing forever, luring and weeping, laugh-
    ing and leaping forever;
Calling forever—calling—for the chase of
    swift wings,
For the drive and the smite of wild wings,
For the fold of strong wings,
For the sleep in warm wings.
Oo-o-roo-o-rrr-ufffff-oo! Thy mother is
    Storm-Dancer, daughter of Winds.
What art thou, Little Chiefling, babe of my
    heart?
The star that I plucked from the mast of
    the night,
When the wings of thy father outstrove me.
Hi-i-ri-i-ki! Ri-eek!
Eagle-Go-High, this is thy son,—
He falls asleep, smiling,

To the scream of thy nesting-call.
Hi-i-ri-i-ki! Ri-i-ki! Ri-eek!

INDIAN LOVER'S HYMN

Sea-Song and Storm-Song
And drums of the night,
Drums of love's footfall beating through
the dark;
Wind of my pulse and a breaking tide,
And my cry the one note, the one note,
Piercing the sky like a star over thee
O See-Gooltha maq-ha-ten-tle,
See-Gooltha with the two high breasts!

I am come as a river between hills,
Meeting the sea among cliffs—
O Waters surging to Waters in the mono-
toned might of the war-chant,
With the sod sounding back,
And thy voice—! sweet to the hunter's ear
Is the shrill arrowed hawk before the wind!
O See-Gooltha maq-ha-ten-tle,
Thy kiss opens the dark
And the moon unfolds in thine eyes.

Thunders of breaking day—
Long foaming surf-lines of light
Sweep the morning beaches,
Blown by winds that march and sing:
Tall winds, with hunters' feet, swift and
trackless,

Scattering the light from Kunaë's * eyes
And the laughter from his mouth—
Red is love's glory on the forest
As a slain moose.
O See-Gooltha maq-ha-ten-tle
I arise from thy heart,
My lips lift, from thy kiss,
Flame-bright wings of new desire spread-
     ing to the Sun.

Give thy hand and leap with me o'er thy
     threshold to the Good Ground!
Run with cool palm to palm pressed,
     breasts beating,
Thighs by fleet thighs flashing, down the
     white swaying shore.
Brown feet and crags and trampling pines,
Tread to the sound,
Of Sea-Song and Storm-Song
And Drums of the Dawn!

THE SONG OF THE HILLS
Being the Song of a Man and a Woman
Who Might Have Loved
(From the Yokut)

This is the song of the Hills
In the hour when they talk together,
When the alpen glow dies down in the west
     and leaves the heavens tender;

* Kunaë: Supreme One.

In the pure and shadowless hour
When the Mountains talk together;

"Fir tree leaneth to fir,
The wind-blown willows mingle;
Clouds draw each to each, dissolve, depart,
        and renew one another;
But the strong Hills hold asunder.

"Had we been less we had loved;
We had stooped and been tender;

"But our hands are under the earth
For the travail of her harvests,
Upholding the rain-sleeked fields
And the long, brown, fruitful furrow.
Terror taketh the earth
When the Mountains move together.

"But ever as winds of Spring
Set the meadow grasses caressing,
And the coo-dove's call.
To the coo-dove's mate
Resounds in the oak-wood valleys,
We shall thrill with the brooding earth,
We shall turn, touch hands, and remember,
Had we been less, how much we had loved
How nobly we might have been tender."

NEITHER SPIRIT NOR BIRD
(*Shoshone Love Song*)

Neither spirit nor bird;
That was my flute you heard
Last night by the River.
When you came with your wicker jar
Where the river drags the willows,
That was my flute you heard,
Wacoba, Wacoba,
Calling, Come to the willows!

Neither the wind nor a bird
Rustled the lupin blooms,
That was my blood you heard
Answer your garment's hem
Whispering through the grasses;
That was my blood you heard
By the wild rose under the willows.

That was no beast that stirred,
That was my heart you heard
Pacing to and fro
In the ambush of my desire,
To the music my flute let fall.
Wacoba, Wacoba,
That was my heart you heard
Leaping under the willows.

PRAYER TO THE MOUNTAIN SPIRIT
(*From the Navajo*)

Lord of the Mountain,
Reared within the Mountain
Young Man, Chieftain,
Hear a young man's prayer!
Hear a prayer for cleanness.
Keeper of the strong rain,
Drumming on the mountain;
Lord of the small rain
That restores the earth in newness;
Keeper of the clean rain,
Hear a prayer for wholeness,

Young Man, Chieftain,
Hear a prayer for fleetness.
Keeper of the deer's way,
Reared among the eagles,
Clear my feet of slothness.
Keeper of the paths of men,
Hear a prayer for straightness.

Hear a prayer for courage.
Lord of the thin peaks,
Reared amid the thunders;
Keeper of the headlands
Holding up the harvest,
Keeper of the strong rocks
Hear a prayer for staunchness.

Young Man, Chieftain,
Spirit of the Mountain!

SONG FOR THE PASSING OF
BEAUTIFUL WOMEN
(*From the Paiute*)

Go thy way in comeliness!
Strong sun across the sod doth make
Such quickening as thy countenance.

Pursue thy unguessed errand and pass by;
I am more worth for what thy passing
    wakes,
Great races in my loins to thee that cry!
My blood is redder for thy loveliness.
Prosper; be fair; pass by!

SONG OF A PASSIONATE LOVER
(*From the Yokut*)

Come not near my songs,
You who are not my lover,
Lest from out that ambush
Leaps my heart upon you!

When my songs are glowing
As an almond thicket
With the bloom upon it,
Lies my heart in ambush
All amid my singing;
Come not near my songs,
You who are not my lover!

Do not hear my songs,
You who are not my lover,

Over-sweet the heart is
Where my love has bruised it,
Breathe you not that fragrance,
You who are not my lover!
Do not stoop above my heart
With its languor on you,
Lest I should not know you
From my own belovèd,
Lest from out my singing
Leaps my heart upon you!

THE HEART'S FRIEND
(*Shoshone Love Song*)

Fair is the white star of twilight,
And the sky clearer
At the day's end;
But she is fairer, and she is dearer
She, my heart's friend!

Fair is the white star of twilight,
And the moon roving
To the sky's end;
But she is fairer, better worth loving,
She, my heart's friend.

A SONG IN TIME OF DEPRESSION
(*From the Paiute*)

Now all my singing Dreams are gone
But none knows where they are fled
Nor by what trail they have left me.

Return, O Dreams of my heart,
And sing in the summer twilight,
By the creek and the almond thicket
And the field that is bordered with lupins!

Now is my refuge to seek
In the hollow of friendly shoulders,
Since the singing is stopped in my pulse
And the earth and the sky refuse me;
Now must I hold by the eyes of a friend
When the high white stars are unfriendly.

Over sweet is the refuge of trusting;
Return and sing, O my Dreams,
In the dewy and palpitant pastures,
Till the love of living awakes
And the strength of the hills to uphold me.

ALONG THE SOUTH STAR TRAIL
(*Tribal Songs from the South-west*)
THE TOM-TOM

Drum-beat, beat of drums,
Pebble-rattle in the gourd,
Pebble feet on drifting sand . . .
Drum-beat, beat of drums—
I have lost the wife-made robe of bear-
skin . . .
Take the prize—mine the loss.
Have I lost too the courage of the black
bear—
His power, his thunder?

Lul-la-by,
Games' queer lullaby . . .
O robe of mine!—
O luck of mine!

   Drum-beat, beat of drums,
Pebble-rattle in the gourd,
Coyote feet upon the plain . . .
Drum-beat, beat of drums—
Coyotes crushed the tender ham-string and
    the bone . . .
A bull-calf bawls, dies alone.
Where are the herds of buffalo and the
    hides,
The meat, the tepees?
Lul-la-by,
Man's dread lullaby . . .
O home of mine!
O life of mine!

   Drum-beat, beat of drums,
Pebble-rattle in the gourd,
Horse-hoof beat upon the ground . . .
Drum-beat, beat of drums—
By Wounded Knee ye buried them, buried
    them—
Red men's flesh, their bones . . .
By Wounded Knee we buried them, buried
    them.
The songs we sung, the dreams . . .
Lul-la-by,

The white man's lullaby . . .
O race of mine!
O brothers mine!

Drum-beat, beat of drums,
Pebble-rattle in the gourd,
Pulse-beat in the fever . . .
Drum-beat, beat of drums—
Famine drank from the gourd bottle, ate
the gourd;
Left the skin, the bone.
She walked the pathway from the east, of
the departed—
Left me forsaken, alone . . .
Lul-la-by,
Tirawa's long lullaby . . .
O blood of mine!
O child of mine!

Drum-beat, beat of drums,
Pebble-rattle in the gourd.
Still feet in the grave-mound . . .
Drum-beat, beat of drums—
The gourd-rattle handle leads to the sun
and life;
Leaves clay, leaves cold.
A purple smoke arises from bowl to float
on winds;
Leaves ashes—my ash . . .
Lul-la-by,
Death's sweet lullaby . . .

O flesh of mine!
O hands of mine!

 Drum-beat, beat of drums,
Pebble-rattle in the gourd,
Dream-feet in the yellow line . . .
Drum-beat, beat of drums—
One half the feather of Tirawa's bird is
  white;
The other black—'tis night;
Tirawa's song at night is morning star of
  dawn
Where dance dreams, in light . . .
Lul-la-by,
The spirit's lullaby . . .
O soul of mine!
O breath of mine!

 Drum-beat, beat of drums,
Pebble-rattle in the gourd,
Calves' feet in starry plains . . .
Drum-beat, beat of drums—
A sacred herd graze on tips of fair fresh
  flowers
In garden—Star of Evening's.
A bison drinks mixed all-waters, pure
From Spring; 'tis hers . . .
Lul-la-by,
All-Life's lullaby . . .
O land of mine!
O plains of mine!

Drum-beat, beat of drums,
Pebble-rattle in the gourd,
Dance-feet 'round the sun . . .
Drum-beat, beat of drums—
By the sun see the dancing white men with
  the red—
By Wounded Knee, a post!
There they blend their songs together,
  brother-wise;
Here the post, the paint . . .
Lul-la-by,
The Nation's lullaby . . .
O race of mine!
O brothers mine!

Drum-beat, beat of drums,
Pebble-rattle in the gourd,
Child feet in the hogan . . .
Drum-beat, beat of drums—
A child has taught her little spider pet to
  weave
Bead-work at my door;
A child has taught these dimming eyes to
  see
Thread-work, star-lit lodge . . .
Lul-la-by,
Love's own lullaby . . .
O hogan mine!
O hogan thine!

Drum-beat, beat of drums,
Pebble-rattle in the gourd,
Soul-feet in trail of wind . . .
Drum-beat, beat of drums—
Hear the great sea-feet, beating on the
    flint-rock!
Drum-beat, beat of drum—
Hear the beat of distant feet on South Star
    Trail!
Drum-beat, beat of drum—
Ti-ra-wa!
Earth's great Ti-ra-wa.
O heart-beat thine!
O drum-beat thine!

SA-A NARAÏ

So I heard it commanded,
On the edge of the mesa,
By the sitter on the mesa,
In the season of falling leaves:

Count thou, my son, the lights on South
    Star Trail;
        Sa-a Naraï
Trust not time nor strength—they are twin
    liars;
        Sa-a Naraï
On track of birth-dance the mourners
    wail—
        Sa-a Naraï

The Tribe moves on—count thou the fires.
Sa-a Naraï
Beads, a few in falling rain; grains in
desert sand;
Sa-a Naraï
The door of night swings wide—it will not
close.
Sa-a Naraï
Still room for beads, dying hills for land;
Sa-a Naraï
The door is open—the Soul Trail glows.
Sa-a Naraï
I counted my sheep but not the bones;
Sa-a Naraï
A woman vows and goes her way;
Sa-a Naraï
Dust-wedded wealth—the desert owns—
Sa-a Naraï
Tomorrow smiles, while sad is yesterday.
Sa-a Naraï
Feast on wit and beauty—pendants of
bone—
Sa-a Naraï
The eye-strings tie two souls today.
Sa-a Naraï
Fill the earthen bowl—fill jar of stone—
Sa-a Naraï
Youth blooms fresh—spring has not gone;
Sa-a Naraï

Winter gathers, gathers fruit of spring
    shower;
       Sa-a Naraï
The frost-chain shakes—a soul moves on.
       Sa-a Naraï
I saw a cripple, I saw a thief.
       Sa-a Naraï
Go, hoe your corn with shoulder-blade of
    deer.
       Sa-a Naraï
Where blows a wind, there stirs a leaf;
       Sa-a Naraï
A bone enghosts a hoe—greed your spear.
       Sa-a Naraï
If Red Moccasin moans, who knows the
    way?
       Sa-a Naraï
I am ashamed before that standing within
    me—
       Sa-a Naraï
The spirit upward flies—it will not stay;
       Sa-a Naraï
Follow soon, thou must, the Voice within
    thee.
       Sa-a Naraï
Shagwakwa laughs—in black night sings—
       Sa-a Naraï
Give me my mother's bones—unto me,
    dreams!
       Sa-a Naraï

A puff to the gods whither blue smoke
   wings—
         Sa-a Naraï
Smoke now with me—soon the yellow line
   gleams.
         Sa-a Naraï
Eat thy mother's flesh—she is the corn:
         Sa-a Naraï
Is there a stranger who is not thy brother?
         Sa-a Naraï
The One Above sung life—lo, love was
   born!
         Sa-a Naraï
Hast shared the gift of thy first mother?
         Sa-a Naraï
A little puff—a little kernel—
         Sa-a Naraï
The Tribe moves on—it will not stay.
         Sa-a Naraï
A little play by the trail eternal—
         Sa-a Naraï
A little puff—lo, the South Star Way . . .

So I heard it chanted.

ON THE WAR-PATH

   Hey—ye!
Hey!
Hey—now go, gather, gather living arrows,
   gather!

Stand ye in the white dawn—
Crouch, spring, run!
Hey now, plume feather, feather—eagle
    flying feather—
Strike ye in the red dawn!
Crouch, spring, run!
Hey, now pray power of storm!
Hey, now pray lightning's bolt!
Hey, now pray power of flint!
Hey, now pray weather, weather—war-like
    stormy weather!
Slay ye in the yellow dawn—
Crouch, spring, run!
Hey, now go, gather, gather, bleeding bon-
    nets gather—huh!

EARTH-MOTHER

O, ho, yo,
O, ho, yo,
To thee, my life,
To thee, my wife,
To thee, my mother—

Who are these the many-feeding?
Heaps of horns,
Hills of fur—
To thee, I come to partake of food,
My mother,
O, ho—

So say'th the spring,
So say'th the wing,
So say'th my mother—

Thus, it was I heard the feet beat—
My ear down,
On the ground—
Yea, I put my lips to thee and drank song,
My mother,
O, ho—

So cries the tree,
So cries the sea,
So cries my mother—

There, the word was overheard,
By the cactus
Standing lone—
Yea, by the cypress thou wilt teach me,
My mother,
O, ho—

So walks the light,
So walks the night,
So walks my mother—

Even unto the long black shadows,
Goeth the frail thing,
Evening star—

Whither thou goeth and thy smile go I,
My mother.
O, ho—

So broods the dark,
So broods the bark,
So broods my mother—

Beneath the bark-blanket were the little
    men—
The six-legged,
Painted black and red—
Unto thee will I hide me to sleep,
My mother,
O, ho—

To thee, O breath,
To thee, O death,
To thee, my mother—

I saw it, yea in a dream, I saw it—
My soul
Arise from sleep—
In the morning, thou wilt call me,
My mother.

O, ho, yo,
O, ho, yo,
To thee, O—
Yo.

FEAST OF WOLVES

Ho, oh-o-o
Come ye shades, shadows come
Ho, oh-o-o
Come ye shades, shadows come
Come ye shades, oh-o-o, ho, oh-o-o
Ye night ghosts and dance ye
What—dark!
Ho, oh-o-o
Come ye wolves, wolf-howls come
Ho, oh-o-o
Come ye wolves, wolf-howls come
Come ye wolves, oh-o-o, ho, oh-o-o
Ye singers merry feast ye
What—bark!
Ho, oh-o-o
Come ye crows, crow-bills come
Ho, oh-o-o
Come ye crows, crow-bills come
Come ye crows, oh-o-o, ho, oh-o-o
Ye black robes and flap ye
What—hark!
Ho, oh-o-o
Come ye bones, bone-grins come
Come ye bones, oh-o-o, ho, oh-o-o
What—stark!

LONE-DOG UNTO THE DELAWARES

Brothers—Lennapi,
Hear ye, come ye, all ye—

By south-way, east-way, shore-land place,
Men come,
Boats come,
Float fast,
Handsome.
Man-who-Paints, much-talker, he much-
    walked
Easterly, south also,
All-time stalked—
Friends they, he says,
Sun-rise men, sun-born men, east-coming;
Great things have, wonderful, thunder-
    ing—
Yea, great things, hear we, from clam-
    clam-sea—
Hear ye—
White-bird boat, great eagle, floats up
    streams,
Man-carrying, house-bearing, much-fire
    gleams.
Friends they,
Say they,
Come ye, hear ye, all ye,
Brothers there, cousins there, Lennapi,
Turtle men, turkey men, wolf clan,
Let us running-friendly be,
Let us brother-hearted be,
Giver-brothers standing we,
Men with meat, men with hides, everyman,
Come ye, run ye, all ye.

From Branchy-river-place,
From Straightened-river-place,
From Great-falls-at,
From Shore-land-at,
Sassafras-land.
Many caves men,
Riding waves men,
All ye Wolves, Turtles, Lennapi—
Bring your gifts, laying them
At Clam-clam-sea.

LISTENING*

The noise of passing feet
On the prairie—
Is it men or gods
Who come out of the silence?

BUFFALO DANCE

Strike ye our land
With curved horns!
Now with cries
Bending our bodies,
Breathe fire upon us;
Now with feet
Trampling the earth,
Let your hoofs
Thunder over us!

*Miss Frances Densmore's literal translations from the Chippewa furnished the keynotes of this and the following five songs.   A. C. H.

Strike ye our land
With curved horns!

WHERE THE FIGHT WAS
In the place where the fight was
Across the river,
In the place where the fight was
Across the river:
A heavy load for a woman
To lift in her blanket,
A heavy load for a woman
To carry on her shoulder.
In the place where the fight was
Across the river,
In the place where the fight was
Across the river:
The women go wailing
To gather the wounded,
The women go wailing
To pick up the dead.

THE WIND
The wind is carrying me round the sky;
The wind is carrying me round the sky.
My body is here in the valley—
The wind is carrying me round the sky.

COURTSHIP
When I go I will give you surely
What you will wear if you go with me;

A blanket of red and a bright girdle,
Two new moccasins and a silver necklace.
When I go I will give you surely
What you will wear if you go with me!

PARTING

Now I go, do not weep, woman—
Woman, do not weep;
Though I go from you to die,
We shall both lie down
At the foot of the hill, and sleep.

Now I go, do not weep, woman—
Woman, do not weep;
Earth is our mother and our tent the sky.
Though I go from you to die,
We shall both lie down
At the foot of the hill, and sleep.

THE LOST LAGOON

It is dusk on the Lost Lagoon,
And we two dreaming the dusk away,
Beneath the drift of a twilight gray—
Beneath the drowse of an ending day
And the curve of a golden moon.

It is dark on the Lost Lagoon,
And gone are the depths of haunting blue,
The grouping gulls, and the old canoe,
The singing firs, and the dusk and—you,
And gone is the golden moon.

O lure of the Lost Lagoon—
I dream tonight that my paddle blurs
The purple shade where the seaweed stirs—
I hear the call of the singing firs
In the hush of the golden moon.

THE SONG MY PADDLE SINGS

West wind, blow from your prairie nest,
Blow from the mountains, blow from the
     west.
The sail is idle, the sailor too;
O! wind of the west, we wait for you.
Blow, blow!
I have wooed you so,
But never a favor you bestow.
You rock your cradle the hills between,
But scorn to notice my white lateen.

I stow the sail, unship the mast:
I wooed you long but my wooing's past;
My paddle will lull you into rest.
O! drowsy wind of the drowsy west,
Sleep, sleep,
By your mountain steep,
Or down where the prairie grasses sweep!
Now fold in slumber your laggard wings,
For soft is the song my paddle sings.

August is laughing across the sky,
Laughing while paddle, canoe and I,
Drift, drift,

Where the hills uplift
On either side of the current swift.
The river rolls in its rocky bed;
My paddle is plying its way ahead;
Dip, dip,
While the waters flip
In foam as over their breast we slip.

And oh, the river runs swifter now;
The eddies circle about my bow.
Swirl, swirl!
How the ripples curl
In many a dangerous pool awhirl!

And forward far the rapids roar,
Fretting their margin for evermore.
Dash, dash,
With a mighty crash,
They seethe, and boil, and bound, and
    splash.

Be strong, O paddle! be brave, canoe!
The reckless waves you must plunge into.
Reel, reel.
On your trembling keel,
But never a fear my craft will feel.

We've raced the rapid, we're far ahead!
The river slips through its silent bed.
Sway, sway,

As bubbles spray
And fall in tinkling tunes away.
And up on the hills against the sky,
A fir tree rocking its lullaby,
Swings, swings,
Its emerald wings,
Swelling the song that my paddle sings.

PLEM-SALIA-KWI

(*Autumn Dawn*)

Plem-Salia-Kwi is the Hunter returning
    with plenty,
And the Fisher from the green sea.
His shoulders are heavy with deer's meat;
His great canoe is slow with salmon.
We listen to the nudge of its tall ghost-
    prow
In all our landing coves.
We hear the ground-wind of his moccasins
Rustling the forest-floors:
Swifter than joy they speed on the purple
    paths of the Fall—
Paths stained with fruitage, oozing odors.
He comes to us, his little brown blood-
    brothers by the sea:—
Through the dark silver-blue spruces, and
    the massed sea-green cedars,
Through the brown and crimson maples,

And the cottonwoods' dropping gold;

Through the pearl shimmer of the naked
    birches.

Plem-Salia-Kwi's blanket is the white,
    broidered, mist;

Its fringes are dew-bells

That tinkle little whispers down the moun-
    tain.

While he still slept,

Lake-Woman, Mother of Waters, wove him
    his blanket:

Wove it of the wool of the mist-herds

Drifting down from the cloud-ranges.

She patterned it in bead-drops, sun-col-
    ored—

A rainbow starts in the heart of each—

With blue ravelings from sky-patches,

With pink shells from the beaches of morn-
    ing.

He bears the strong bent bow of the hills,

And the swift wind-arrows scarlet-shafted
    with dawn:

And the tall spear of falling light,

October light, the mystical weapon.

[Ah-h! Ahi! Ah-h! We sing to Kunaë

For the beauty and harvest of Plem-Salia-
    Kwi.]

The little children,

In laughing, leaping, running, stumbling,

Pattering and creeping down to the
  beaches,
Give thanks for the harvest of sweet, dried,
  berries
And the plenty of the breast.
They go down to converse with the swal-
  lows,
Who bathe in the small leaf-locked pools.
Ak-hi! the shrill joy of the children,
At the twirring and flashing of brown wings
  in bright water,
And the twittering of news from all the
  nests of the sea-coast!

The pine-logs make a good smoke, blue,
  clear, sweet-smelling,
The cooking baskets bubble with water:
The women chant, while they heat stones
  for the baking,
Concerning the large baskets of food they
  have cooked,
And the racks of crimson, smoked salmon,
And the many trays of dried berries,
Sun-baked and jellied in long strips, packed
  in cool leaves.
They behold their men coming up from the
  caves
With hammers and copper, with silver and
  cunning shells;
And they clatter at their ears, saying:—

"Is not thy roof fragrant with cedar-trays
of berries?
Have I not stored thy house full?
Hast thou not a little wayward son of thee
at each of thy hands?
Is the cradle on my back—the cradle of thy
despised little daughter—empty?
Where is another such wife?
Speak, O thou Hunter of Life,
That caughtest me unknowing in the pine
shadows—
Ak-hi-i! Il-ak-il-ak!—
When I danced after Tem-Eyos-Kwi!"

The men answer not:
But in their eyes, behind their lashes, is a
little smile,
Like light in the depths of a reedy pool.
Early, ere their clattering women woke,
They went down to the caves with their
axes.
They have digged copper and silver and
brilliant shells
From a secret store.
Tink-tonk, tink-tonk, tink-tonk!
Through the forest rings the song of their
hammers.
The silent men are hammering rings for
their women:

Rings, bracelets, anklets, for their women,
Glad gifts for their women, their mates.

For the silent men have seen
That Plem-Salia-Kwi walks not alone.
Through all his paths She follows him—
    his Woman, his Mate—
Sharing his blanket.
She has no other garment, her breast is
    bare,
She has given all to him she follows;
So comes he with plenty!
He tires not forever on his leagues of
    march,
Because her feet are set to his foot-prints,
And the gleam of her bare hand slants
    across his shoulder.
Therefore the silent men, the Hunters and
    Providers of Life,
Greet   Plem-Salia-Kwi,   the   Harvest-
    Bringer, their Blood-Brother the
    Mated One,
With the tink-tonk, tink-tonk, tink-tonk of
    bright hammers,
Shaping gifts for their women:
Ringing their thanksgiving song for full
    joys—
Full baskets, full cradles, the full arms of
    sleep.

SONGS FROM THE HAKO:
A PAWNEE CEREMONY

Rendered in the rhythms of the originals

by

Alice Fletcher

With interpretations by Tahirussawichi,
a Pawnee

PREFATORY NOTE

The position of Tahirussawichi in the Pawnee tribe is that of a man worthy of respect—one versed in a knowledge of serious things, whose life has been devoted to the acquisition and maintenance of certain sacred rites. He is esteemed as a man of truth—one who has the favor of Tirawa. He possesses a knowledge of curative roots, and often attends the sick, using herbs as medicine. He is the keeper of certain old and sacred objects, and leads in their attendant ceremonies. His great care in observing all the details of the intricate ceremony of the Hako is well known in the tribe, and much good fortune is believed to follow his leadership in this ceremony. His title is Kurahus. This term is applied to a man of years who has been instructed in the meaning and use of sacred objects as well as their ceremonies. The word is sometimes employed as a synonym for a venerable man, one who commands respect, but throughout this paper it is used in its official sense—the leader of the ceremony.

Nature of the Ceremony

The teachings of the public ceremony were general in character. They emphasized, on the one hand, man's dependence on the supernatural for all the gifts of life, and on the other hand, his dependence on the family tie for the gifts of peace and happiness. The specific teachings were reserved for the Son. These began in the ritual to the Dawn (tenth ritual) on the morning of the second and third days, which prefigured the secret ceremonies of the fifth morning, when the bond of the family relation was extended beyond blood kinship through the symbolic rites which recognized the common source of life in Tirawa atius.

Looking over the entire ceremony, it is interesting to note how older rites have had their share in the development of the Hako, and how the trend of thought among the native seers has borne them toward a conception of the brotherhood of man, a conception recognized as the noblest known to the human family.

This impressive ritual-drama may be compared to a medieval Miracle Play, and has exercised an influence no less profound on the tribes which have performed it. The chief persons in the drama are, the Father, the Son, the Children, and attendant Deities (the associates and representatives of Tirawa atius, the Master of Life). Mother Corn, Kawas, the Eagle, the Morning Star, the Dawn, the Day and Father Sun. The Father is chosen from the tribe which presents the great spectacle; the Son is selected by the priests from another tribe by the curious psychic process described in the Second Ritual. Unusual blessings are supposed to accrue to those who take the leading parts.

THE HAKO: A PAWNEE CEREMONY

FIRST RITUAL

INVOKING THE POWERS

Explanation by the Kurahus, or Chief Priest

At the creation of the world it was arranged that there should be lesser powers. Tirawa atius, the mighty power, could not come near to man, could not be seen or felt by him, therefore lesser powers were permitted. They were to mediate between man and Tirawa. The first song mentions some of these lesser powers in the order in which they come near to man, in the order of their creation.

Invocation to the Great Spirits

I

We heed as unto thee we call;
Oh, send to us thy potent aid!

253

Help us, Oh, holy place above!
We heed as unto thee we call.

II

We heed as unto thee we call;
Oh, send to us thy potent aid!
Help us, Hotoru, giver of breath!
We heed as unto thee we call.

III

We heed as unto thee we call;
Oh, send to us thy potent aid!
Help us, Shakuru, father of strength!
We heed as unto thee we call.

IV

We heed as unto thee we call;
Oh, send to us thy potent aid!
Help us, h'Uraru, mother of all!
We heed as unto thee we call.

PREPARING THE FEATHERED STEM

Blue is the color of the sky, the dwelling place of Tirawahut, that great circle of the powers which watch over man. As the man paints the stick blue we sing. We ask as we sing that life be given to this symbol of the dwelling place of Tirawa.

We paint the groove red because the passageway is red through which man's breath comes and goes to give him life. The sun, too, is red, and the groove represents the straight path whereon the sun shines, the

path which man must travel if he would live
in peace and prosper. The teachings of
this ceremony make a straight path along
which if a man walks he will receive help
from the powers.

I

Take we now the blue paint,
Touch with it the stem, putting on the
      sacred symbol,
Emblem of the clear sky,
Where dwell the gods, who, descending,
      bring us good gifts,
Gifts of life and plenty.

II

When the man begins to paint the stick
green this song is sung.

Take we now the green paint,
Touch with it the stem, the mated stem,
Putting on the emblem, the sacred and liv-
      ing symbol.
Mother earth.
From above descending, bountiful blessings
      on thee,
Mother earth.

Oh, Kawas, come, with wings outspread in
      sunny skies!

Oh, Kawas, come, and bring us peace, thy
    gentle peace!
Oh, Kawas, come, and give new life to us
    who pray!

In this ceremony the brown eagle is
called Kawas. This eagle has been made
holy by being sacrificed to Tirawa. Its
feathers are tied upon the stem that has
been painted blue to represent the sky.

This stem was the first one painted and
decorated, because it is female and the
leader. It represents the night, the moon,
the north, and stands for kindness and help-
fulness. It will take care of the people. It
is the mother.

Throughout the ceremony the Kurahus
carries this feathered stem.

SONG TO MOTHER CORN

Mother Corn knows all places and all
that happens among men; therefore the
corn which comes from her must lead, must
direct us where to go.

I

Tirawa, harken! Mighty one,
Above us in blue, silent sky!
We standing wait thy bidding here.
The Mother Corn standing waits,

Waits to serve thee here;
The Mother Corn stands waiting here.

II

Tirawa, harken! Mighty one,
Above us in blue, silent sky!
We flying seek thy dwelling there.
The Mother Corn flying goes
Up to seek thee there;
The Mother Corn goes flying up.

III

Tirawa, harken! Mighty one,
Above us in blue, silent sky!
Behold! We in thy dwelling stand.
The Mother Corn, standing there.
Leader she is made;
The Mother Corn is leader made.

IV

Tirawa, harken! Mighty one,
Above us in blue, silent sky!
The downward path we take again.
The Mother Corn, leading us,
Doth thy symbol bear;
The Mother Corn with power leads.

Mother Corn having reached the blue dome where dwells the great circle of powers, Tirawahut, and having gained what she went for, tawitshpa, authority to lead in the ceremony, she descends to earth by the four paths.

SECOND RITUAL

PREFIGURING THE JOURNEY TO THE SON

The spirit of Mother Corn leads our
spirits in the search for the Son. We
draw near, in the spirit, to the village
where the Son dwells. The Son does not
see us as we stand there; he is sleeping.
We fix our minds upon Mother Corn and
upon him; we think of the gifts we are to
bring him when we come to him with the
Hako, the gifts that the birds and the ani-
mals that attend these sacred objects will
surely bestow upon him—long life, chil-
dren, and plenty. Now the spirit of
Mother Corn touches him.

We fix our minds upon Mother Corn
and upon the Son; if we are in earnest he
will respond to her touch. He will not
waken, he will not see her, but he will see
in a dream that which her touch will bring
to him, one of the birds that attend the
Hako, for all the spirits of those birds are
with Mother Corn and they do her bidding,
and he may hear the bird call to him. Then,
when he awakens, he will remember his
dream, and as he thinks upon it, he will
know that he has been chosen to be a Son,
and that all the good things that come with

the ceremony which will make him a Son
are now promised to him.

I

Chant of the Mystic Journey

Mother Corn, Oh hear! Open our way!
Lo! As we draw near, let our souls touch
    thine
While we pray thee:
Children give to us. Mother Corn, hear!

II

Mother Corn, Oh hear! Open our way!
Lo! Our heads we bow, while our souls
    touch thine;
Then as one mind
Make the choice of Son. Mother Corn,
    hear!

III

Mother Corn, Oh hear! Open our way!
Lo! With head erect Mother stands, and
    then
Moves she through air
On her mission bent. Mother Corn, hear!

IV

Mother Corn, Oh hear! Open our way!
Lo! Now over hills, over streams, we go
Taking our way
Toward the Children's land. Mother Corn,
    hear!

V

Mother Corn, Oh hear! Open our way!

Lo! Our journey's end now is near, we
    look
O'er the strange land,
Seeking Children there! Mother Corn,
    hear!

VI

Mother Corn, Oh hear! Open our way!
Lo! Our eyes behold where they dwell. In
    their
Village we walk,
Seeking there the Son. Mother Corn, hear!

VII

Mother Corn, Oh hear! Open our way!
Lo! His lodge we find, through the door
    we pass.
Sleeping he lies,
Knows not we are there. Mother Corn,
    hear!

VIII

Mother Corn, Oh hear! Open our way!
Lo! Now at her touch comes a dream;
    then a
Bird calls, "My son!"
While his soul responds. Mother Corn,
    hear!

THIRD RITUAL

SENDING THE MESSENGERS

The four messengers are selected infor-
mally by the Father from among his near

relatives. They are generally young men,
lithe and strong of limb, and able to make
a long journey quickly. The distance to be
traveled varies from a few miles to a hun-
dred or more, and as they must carry all
their provisions, it becomes necessary for
them to get over the ground as rapidly as
possible.

The formal appointment of these mes-
sengers takes place in the lodge of the
Father, in the presence of the sacred ob-
jects spread at ceremonial rest.

When the messengers arrive at the lodge
of the Son, he sends for his kindred and
consults with them. Only a recent death in
his family or some catastrophe which has
deprived him of his property will be ac-
cepted as sufficient excuse for his not re-
ceiving the Hako party. If he accepts the
tobacco he will bid the messengers return
to the Father and say, "I am ready." In
either case he must make gifts to the mes-
sengers in recognition of the proffered
honor.

I

The Father's Message to the Son

I bid you travel o'er the land to the Son,
And with you take these words of mine
    unto him:

"Behold! Your Father comes to you
speedily."

II

We wait their journey o'er the land to the
Son,
When they will give these words of mine
unto him:
"Behold! Your Father comes to you
speedily."

FOURTH RITUAL
VIVIFYING THE SACRED OBJECTS

On the morning of the day the journey
is to begin the Kurahus rises from his
place in the lodge behind the Hako and goes
outside. There he ties the sacred objects
on the selected tent pole.

The rope of buffalo hair is used to tie
these sacred objects to the pole, which is
then set up at the entrance of the lodge.
Here it stands where the wind of the dawn
may breathe upon the Hako and the first
rays of the sun strike the sacred objects
and give them life.

Song of Praise to Mother Corn

As we sing we think that Mother breath-
ing forth life, who has come out of the
past, has now started to lead us on the

journey we are to take and to the fulfil-
ment of our desire that children may be
given us, that generations may not fail in
the future, and that the tie may be made
strong between the Father and the Son.

I

Mother with the life-giving power now
    comes,
Stepping out of far distant days she comes,
Days wherein to our fathers gave she food;
As to them, so now unto us she gives,
Thus she will to our children faithful be.
Mother with the life-giving power now
    comes!

II

Mother with the life-giving power is here.
Stepping out of far distant days she comes.
Now she forward moves, leading as we
    walk
Toward the future, where blessings she
    will give,
Gifts for which we have prayed granting
    to us.
Mother with the life-giving power is here!

THE HAKO PARTY PRESENTED TO THE POWERS
Invocation to Tirawa

This song is addressed to Tirawa atius.
He is the father of all and all things come

from him. We pray in our hearts as we
sing. We ask Tirawa to watch over the
Kurahus, to guide his acts and to guard his
words so that he may make no mistake and
the ceremony may be complete. From the
east the flashes of the eyes of Tirawa come
darting through the air upon us and upon
the sacred objects.

Look on us as here we are standing, raising
  our voices!
Look on us as here we, presenting, lift now
  these emblems that are so holy up to
  thy gaze!
Swift, a flash from out of the heavens
Falls on us as here we are standing, look-
  ing at thee.

Invocation to the Gods

The people are now looking toward the
north, the moon, the night, the mother of
the day.

We ask the powers of the north, they
who can see the path of life, to lead us and
make us able to walk, us and our children.

To all the powers of the east, west,
south, and north we have sung and have
presented ourselves. As we walked, we
have traced upon the earth the figure of a
man. This image that we have traced is

from Tirawa. It has gone around with us,
and its feet are where we now stand; its
feet are with our feet and will move with
them as we now take four steps, bearing
the sacred objects, in the presence of all
the powers and begin our journey to the
land of the Son.

I

Look down, West gods, look upon us! We
    gaze afar on your dwelling.
Look down while here we are standing, look
    down upon us, ye mighty!
Ye thunder gods, now behold us!
Ye lightning gods, now behold us!
Ye that bring life, now behold us!
Ye that bring death, now behold us!

II

Look down, South gods, look upon us! We
    gaze afar on your dwelling.
Look down while here we are standing,
    look down upon us, ye mighty!
Ye daylight gods, now behold us!
Ye sunshine gods, now behold us!
Ye increase gods, now behold us!
Ye plenty gods, now behold us.

III

Look down, North gods, look upon us! We
    gaze afar on your dwelling.
    look down upon us, ye mighty!
Ye darkness gods, now behold us!

Ye moonlight gods, now behold us!
Ye that direct, now behold us!
Ye that discern, now behold us!

FIFTH RITUAL

MOTHER CORN ASSERTS
AUTHORITY
The Journey Begins

I

The mother leads and we follow on,
Her devious pathway before us lies.
She leads us as were our fathers led
Down through the ages.

II

The mother leads us and we follow on,
Her pathway straight, where a stage each
    day
We forward walk, as our fathers walked
Down through the ages.

Mother Corn, who led our spirits over
the path we are now to travel, leads us
again as we walk, in our bodies, over the
land.

We speak of this path as devious, not
merely because we must go over hills and
through valleys and wind around gulches
to reach the land of the Son, but because
we are thinking of the way by which,

through the Hako, we can make a man who is not of our blood a Son; a way which has come down to us from our far-away ancestors like a winding path.

Crossing the Prairie

I

Looking o'er the prairie, naught our eyes
 discern there,
Wide the land stretches out before us;
Then we cry aloud to Mother Corn: "Doth
 thy pathway lie here?"

II

Heeding now our crying, while our eyes
 she opens,
Mother Corn moveth out before us
On the lonely prairie, where we see straight
 the pathway lies there!

Song of Obedience

Mother Corn speaks to us and we are assured in our spirits. The next song is to enforce obedience to Mother Corn.

I

Hark! She speaks, and quickly we turn to
 her,
Looking toward the west to the spot where
 we
Passed 'neath the eyes of gods; and now do
 we heed her words:

"Yonder is the place in the distant west
Whence I have come out of the past to
    you."

II

"Born of the earth and touched by the deep
    blue sky,
Have I chosen been by the gods to lead.
You are to hear my voice and follow my
    strict commands,
As your fathers did in the days gone by.
Thence come I to open your pathway here."

SONGS AND CEREMONIES OF THE WAY

The journey we are taking is for a sacred
purpose, and as we are led by the super-
natural power in Mother Corn we must ad-
dress with song every object we meet, be-
cause Tiráwa is in all things. Everything
we come to as we travel can give us help,
and send help by us to the Children.

Trees are among the lesser powers, and
they are represented on the Hako which we
carry, so when we see trees we must sing
to them.

Trees grow along the banks of the
streams; we can see them at a distance, like
a long line, and we can see the river glisten-
ing in the sunlight in its length. We sing
to the river, and when we come nearer and

see the water and hear it rippling, then we
sing to the water, the water that ripples as
it runs.

Song to the Trees and Streams
I
Dark against the sky yonder distant line
Lies before us.   Trees we see, long the line
    of trees,
Bending, swaying in the breeze.
II
Bright with flashing light yonder distant
    line
Runs before us, swiftly runs, swift the river
    runs,
Winding, flowing o'er the land.
III
Hark.   Oh, hark.   A sound, yonder distant
    sound
Comes to greet us, singing comes, soft the
    river's song,
Rippling gently 'neath the trees.

Song When Crossing the Streams
I
Behold, upon the river's brink we stand!
River we must cross;
Oh, Kawas, come!   To thee we call.   Oh,
    come, and thy permission give
Into the stream to wade and forward go.

II

Behold, the water covers now our feet!
River we must cross;
Oh, Kawas, hear! To thee we call. Oh,
    come, and thy permission give
On through the stream to pass and forward
    go.

Song to the Wind

I

Hither, Winds, come to us, touch where
    water
O'er us flowed when we waded;
Come, oh, Winds, come!

II

Lo! The Winds round us sweep where
    water
O'er us flowed. Safe now are we,
By the Winds safe.

Song to the Mountains

I

Mountains loom upon the path we take;
Yonder peak now rises sharp and clear;
Behold! It stands with its head uplifted,
Thither go we, since our way lies there.

II

Mountains loom upon the path we take;
Yonder peak now rises sharp and clear;
Behold! We climb, drawing near its sum-
    mit;
Steeper grows the way and slow our steps.

III
Mountains loom upon the path we take;
Yonder peak that rises sharp and clear,
Behold us now on its head uplifted;
Planting there our feet, we stand secure.

IV
Mountains loom upon the path we take;
Yonder peak that rose so sharp and clear,
Behold us now on its head uplifted;
Resting there at last, we sing our song.

Song to the Mesa

I
The mesa see; its flat top like a straight line
    cuts across the sky;
It blocks our path, and we must climb, the
    mesa climb.

II
More mesas see; their flat tops rise against
    the sky, they bar our path;
We reach their base, and we must climb, the
    mesas climb.

III
The mesas' side we now ascend, the sharp
    ridge pass, its flat top reach;
There lies their base that we must take, and
    forward go.

IV
The mesas rise around us still, their flat
    tops cut across the sky:

They block our way, yet still we climb, the
mesas climb.

MOTHER CORN REASSERTS LEADERSHIP

The Search for the Children

I

Here we give our thanks, led by Mother
Corn,

As our eyes dwell upon the borders of the
land

Where dwell the Children we are seeking.

II

Now our eyes look on people walking to.

Soon our eyes catch the print of footsteps
on the ground,

Made by the Children we are seeking.

III

Still we travel on, led by Mother Corn.

Now our eyes look on people walking to
and fro;

They the Children are, we are seeking.

As we move on and enter the land of the
Children we sing, in the second stanza,
about their footprints, the marks of their
moccasins where they have walked to and
fro on the ground.

We may not actually see these marks, but
the song represents us as seeing them;

Mother Corn has seen them, and she is lead-
ing us.

When the village of the Children is in
sight the following song is sung. Mother
Corn speaks in the first stanza and tells us
she has come again to this place. Her
spirit had been here before when she came
seeking the Son. To-day we have arrived
with her at this her destination, and we give
thanks to Mother Corn.

Song of the Journey's End
I
Here is the place where I came, seeking to
    find the Son;
Here have I led you again, here is our jour-
    ney's end.
Thanks we give unto the Mother Corn!
Here is the place where she came, seeking
    to find the Son;
Here she has led us again, here is our jour-
    ney's end.
II
Here to this place have we come, bringing
    the Son our gifts,
All of the gifts that go forth bearing the
    promised help.
Thanks he'll give as he sees, Mother Corn,
All of the gifts that we bring, bring to his
    village here;

Here, where you led, Mother **Corn; here,**
    where our journey ends.

SIXTH RITUAL

THE SON'S MESSAGES RECEIVED

I

Now our eyes look on him who is here;
He is as the Son we have sought;
He brings again tidings from the Son:
"Father, come to me, here I sit,
Waiting here for thee."

II

Now our eyes look on him who is clad
As befits the Son we have sought;
He, arising, walks; follow we his steps,
Moving slowly on toward the Son,
Where he waiting sits.

The pack containing the clothing pro-
vided for this representative of the Son is
now opened. After the messenger has fin-
ished eating he is dressed in the new cloth-
ing.

We clothe him because that is an act
which marks the care of a father for his
child. The garments we put upon him are

fine and embroidered; these fine and care-
fully made garments show that we have
been thinking of him, that we regard him
highly and wish to do him honor.

Just before we reach the village we halt
and sing the next song.

Seeking the Son

I

Where is he, the Son?
Where his dwelling place that I seek?
Which can be his lodge, where he sits
Silent, waiting, waiting there for me?

II

Here is he, the Son,
Here is his dwelling place that I seek;
This is here his lodge, where he sits
Silent, waiting, waiting here for me.

SEVENTH RITUAL

THE CONSECRATION OF THE LODGE

When the Son has dispatched his messen-
ger to the Hako party, he with a few of his
near relatives, enters the lodge set apart

for the ceremony, there to await the return of his messenger and the coming of the Fathers.

He seats himself at the south side of the lodge near the door. This is the humblest place, and he takes it to show that he is not seeking his own honor. By the choice of him as the Son a very high honor has been bestowed upon him, and his appreciation of this is shown by his taking the seat of the lowliest and not assuming prominence before the people.

The Kúrahus directs the chief of the Hako party to advance one step and to stand upon the threshold while the first stanza of the next song is sung.

Touching and Crossing the Threshold

I

Sent down by powers on high,
She bears a promise most sure;
The Mother Corn breathes forth life,
On threshold She stands
Of my Son's dwelling. All's well!

II

Sent down by powers on high,
She bears a promise most sure—
Now Kawas, bringing new life,
The threshold crosses
Of my Son's dwelling. All's well!

Mother Corn Breathing Life Is Now Walk-
ing in the Lodge

I

The Mother Corn, with breath of life,
Now enters into my Son's lodge;
There she walks within:
With breath of life walks Mother Corn.
The Mother Corn, with breath of life,
Now circles she within the lodge,
Walking round within;
With breath of life walks Mother Corn.

Kawas Hovers Overhead in the Lodge

I

Kawas, bearing new life, entereth this
dwelling,
Comes as to her own nest, on her spread
pinions;
There so gently she hovers over these her
Children.

II

Kawas, bearing new life, flieth through this
dwelling,
All the lodge she cleanses, with her wings
sweeping,
Making clear the place, sweeping out the
harm and danger.

CLOTHING THE SON AND OFFERING THE SMOKE

The lodge having been made ready as a nest within which life might be given and made secure, the Father performs his first act of recognition and responsibility. He puts upon the Son the garments he has previously prepared for the purpose. When clad in the finely embroidered clothing, the Son is told to make the offering of smoke to Tiráwa atius, as a prayer for the consecration of the new-born relationship.

The Son Prays to the Gods

I

My son, now heed, attend to the command
    I give to you;
Oh, speak to the gods list'ning above us!
Oh, let your prayers ascend to the mighty
    ones on high!

II

My son obeys. His voice is now trav'ling
    far, speeding on;
It goes to the list'ning gods above us;
There will his prayer be heard by the
    mighty ones on high.

Song of the Prayer Smoke
I
See the smoke pass by!
Rising high above, follows where his voice
Sped, intent to reach
Where the gods abide in the deep blue sky.
See the smoke pass by!
II
See the smoke ascend!
Now the odor mounts, follows where his
    voice
Sped, intent to reach
Where the gods abide.   There the odor
    pleads,
Pleads to gain us help.

EIGHTH RITUAL (First Day)

THE FATHERS FEED THE CHILDREN

Now the heralds summon the people to
the lodge and they come, dressed in their
best attire and bringing gifts.

In Praise of Tirawa
Father, unto thee we cry!
Father thou of gods and men;

Father thou of all we hear;
Father thou of all we see—
Father, unto thee we cry!

INVOCATION TO THE ALL-FATHER

When the Kúrahus begins to sing this
song he must think what this ceremony is
for and be mindful that all the powers that
the heavens contain and all the powers that
are felt over the earth are now coming near
and bending over the Hako.

All the powers that are in the heavens
and all those that are upon the earth are
derived from the mighty power, Tiráwa
atius. He is the father of all things visible
and invisible. He is the father of all the
people, and perpetuates the life of the tribe
through the gift of children. So we sing,
your father, meaning the father of all peo-
ple everywhere, the father of all things that
we see and hear and feel.

Father, thou above, father of the gods,
They who can come near and touch us,
Do thou bid them bring us help.
Help we need. Father, hear us!

SONGS FOR LAYING DOWN THE FEATHERED STEMS

First Song

The feathered stems represent the eagle; the holy place, where the stems are laid to rest, represents the eagle's nest. A nest is made for the young; the making of a nest in the lodge of the Son by Kawas presages the fulfilment of the promise of children to the Son, as well as the establishment of a close bond, like that of father and son, between the members of two unrelated clans or tribes.

I

See where she comes to her little one lying
    so snugly and safely the nest in!
Hark! She is calling; hear her,
List as her nestlings make answer;
See how she gently hovers.
Happy our hearts as we look on her hovering over her nestlings so gently.

II

See where she comes to her little ones lying
    so snugly and safely the nest in!
Hark! She is calling; hear her,
List as her nestlings answer;
See her alighting gently.

Happy our hearts as we see her alighting
　　there over her nestlings so gently.

Second Song

I

Loud, loud the young eagles cry, cry, seeing
　　their mother come;
Flies she to them slantwise, flies;
Then over the nest she hangs, there hover-
　　ing, stays her flight;
Thanks, thanks as we look we give.

II

Thanks, thanks, from our hearts we give,
　　thanks give as we watch the bird
As she to them slantwise flies:
Then over her nest she drops; there, fold-
　　ing her wings, she rests,
Rests safely within her nest.

NINTH RITUAL (First Night)

THE VISIONS ARE INVOKED

When the sun has set and it is dark and
the stars are shining, then the Children
gather in the lodge. Some, as they come
in, will advance to the holy place and there
drop a stick; this means the gift of a pony.

For every such gift the Kúrahus returns thanks to the giver.

After all are seated, wood is piled upon the fire, and when the flames leap high the Kúrahus rises, then his assistant and the chief rise and the Hako are taken up.

The singers carrying the drum follow the Hako bearers as they move slowly around the lodge, singing the following song.

I

Holy visions!
Hither come, we pray you, come unto us,
Bringing with you joy;
Come, oh, come to us, holy visions,
Bringing with you joy.

We sing about the visions which the birds on the feathered stems are to bring to the Children.

Visions come from above, they are sent by Tiráwa atius. The lesser powers come to us in visions. We receive help through the visions. All the promises which attend the Hako will be made good to us in this way.

Visions can come most readily at night; spirits travel better at that time. Now when we are met together we, the Fathers, call upon the visions to come to the Children.

II

Holy visions!
Near are they approaching, near to us here,
Bringing with them joy;
Nearer still they come—holy visions—
Bringing with them joy.

The visions have heard the call of the spirits of the birds upon the feathered stems, joined to the call of our spirits, and they are descending by the east from their dwelling place above, and are coming toward the lodge.

We sing, "They are coming," and the Children join in the song, as we pass around and wave the feathered stems.

III

Holy visions!
Lo! Before the doorway pause they, waiting,
Bearing gifts of joy;
Pausing there they wait—holy visions—
Bearing gifts of joy.

As we sing the visions touch and cross the threshold and then pass down the long passageway leading into the lodge. As we reach the west they have entered the lodge.

Kawas and all the birds have called these visions to bless the Children. The visions have heard, they have traveled far, they have reached the lodge, and now they have entered and are in the presence of the Children.

IV

Holy visions!
Now they cross the threshold, gliding softly
Toward the space within;
Softly gliding on—holy visions—
Toward the space within.

V

Holy visions!
They the lodge are filling with their presence,
Fraught with hope and peace;
Filling all the lodge—holy visions
Fraught with hope and peace.

The visions which attend the Hako are now touching the Children, touching them here and there and by their touch giving them dreams, which will bring them health, strength, happiness, and all good things.

VI

Holy visions!
Now they touch the children, gently touch them,
Giving dreams of joy;
Gently touch each one—holy visions—
Giving dreams of joy.

As we sing, the visions are walking away; they have done what they came to do; they are now leaving the lodge, and when we reach the west the space they had filled is empty.

We pause and we think of the visions going away over the silent earth to ascend to their dwelling place.

VII

Holy visions!
Ended now their mission, pass they outward,
Yet they leave us joy;
Pass they all from us—holy visions—
Yet they leave us joy.

VIII

Holy visions!
They, the sky ascending, reach their dwelling;
There they rest above;
They their dwelling reach—holy visions—
There they rest above.

TENTH RITUAL

THE BIRTH OF DAWN

As the night draws to a close, the Kúrahus orders the server to lift the skins which hang at the outer and inner doors of the long passageway of the lodge, and to go outside and watch for the first glimmer of light.

At the first indication of a change, when the air begins to stir, the server comes in with the tidings, and we rise, take up the Hako, and stand at the west, behind the holy place; there, looking toward the east, we sing this song. We sing it slowly and with reverent feeling, for it speaks of the mysterious and powerful act of Tiráwa atius in the birth of Dawn.

The Summons to Mother Corn
I
Awake, Oh, Mother, from sleep!
Awake! The night is far spent;
The signs of dawn are now seen
In east, whence cometh new life.

We call to Mother Earth, who is represented by the ear of corn. She has been asleep and resting during the night. We ask her to awake, to move, to arise, for the signs of the dawn are seen in the east and the breath of the new life is here.

Mother Earth hears the call; she moves, she awakes, she arises, she feels the breath of the new-born Dawn. The leaves and the grass stir; all things move with the breath of the new day; everywhere life is renewed.

This is very mysterious; we are speaking of something very sacred, although it happens every day.

The Awakening of Mother Corn
II

The Mother wakens from sleep;
She wakes, for night is far spent;
The signs of dawn are now seen
In east, whence cometh new life.

The eagle soars where these powers dwell and can communicate with them. The new life of the new day is felt by these powers above as well as by Mother Earth below.

The Summons to Kawas, the Eagle
III

Awake, oh, Kawas, from sleep!
Awake! The night is far spent;
The signs of dawn are now seen
In east, whence cometh new life.

The Awakening of Kawas
IV

Now Kawas wakens from sleep,
Awakes, for night is far spent;
The signs of dawn are now seen
In east, whence cometh new life.

H'Kawas hears the call and awakes. Now all the powers above wake and stir, and all things below wake and stir; the breath of new life is everywhere. With the signs in the east has come this new life.

Kawas, the brown eagle, the messenger of the powers above, now stands within the lodge and speaks. The Kúrahus hears his voice as she tells him what the signs in the east mean.

She tells him that Tiráwa atius there moves upon Darkness, the Night, and causes her to bring forth the Dawn. It is the breath of the new-born Dawn, the child of Night and Tiráwa atius, which is felt by all the powers and all things above and below and which gives them new life for the new day.

V

Then Kawas stands and speaks forth:
"A child from Night is now born;
Tiráwa, father on high,
On Darkness moving, brings Dawn."

VI

I understand now, I know
A child from Night has been born;
Tiráwa, father on high,
On Darkness moving, brings Dawn."

THE MORNING STAR AND THE NEW-BORN DAY

We sing this song slowly with reverent feeling, for we are singing of very sacred things.

The Morning Star is like a man; he is painted red all over; that is the color of life. He is clad in leggins and a robe is wrapped about him. On his head is a soft downy eagle's feather, painted red. This feather represents the soft, light cloud that is high in the heavens, and the red is the touch of a ray of the coming sun. The soft, downy feather is the symbol of breath and life.

The star comes from a great distance, too far away for us to see the place where it starts. At first we can hardly see it; we lose sight of it, it is so far off; then we see it again, for it is coming steadily toward us all the time. We watch it approach; it comes nearer and nearer; its light grows brighter and brighter.

Invocation to the Morning Star

I

Oh, Morning Star, for thee we watch!
Dimly comes thy light from distant skies;

We see thee, then lost thou art.
Morning Star, thou bringest life to us.

II

Oh, Morning Star, thy form we see!
Clad in shining garments dost thou come,
Thy plume touched with rosy light.
Morning Star, thou now art vanishing.

Invocation to Dawn

III

Oh, youthful Dawn, for thee we watch!
Dimly comes thy light from distant skies;
We see thee, then lost art thou.
Youthful Dawn, thou bringest life to us.

IV

Oh, youthful Dawn, we see thee come!
Brighter grows thy glowing light
As near, nearer thou dost come.
Youthful Dawn, thou now art vanishing.

As we sing this song the Morning Star comes still nearer and now we see him standing there in the heavens, a strong man shining brighter and brighter. The soft plume in his hair moves with the breath of the new day, and the ray of the sun touches it with color. As he stands there so bright, he is bringing us strength and new life.

As we look upon him he grows less

bright, he is receding, going back to his dwelling place whence he came. We watch him vanishing, passing out of our sight. He has left with us the gift of life which Tiráwa atius sent him to bestow.

As we stand, looking through the long passageway of the lodge, watching and singing, we see the Dawn come nearer and nearer; its brightness fills the sky, the shadowy forms on the earth are becoming visible. As we watch, the Dawn, like the Morning Star, recedes. It is following the Star, going back to the place whence it came, to its birthplace.

The Day is close behind, advancing along the path of the Morning Star and, as we watch, the Dawn vanishes from our sight.

DAYLIGHT

We sing this song with loud voices, we are glad. We shout, "Daylight has come! Day is here!" The light is over the earth. As we look out through the door of the lodge we can see the trees, and all things stand out clearly in the light.

We call to the Children, we bid them awake and throw off the robes that covered their heads as they slept and let their eyes

look out and behold the light of day, the
day that has come, that is here.

Song of the Joy of Day
I
Day is here! Day is here, is here!
Arise, my son, lift thine eyes. Day is here!
  Day is here, is here!
Day is here! Day is here, is here!
Look up, my son, and see the day. Day is
  here! Day is here, is here!
Day is here! Day is here, is here!
II
Lo, the deer! Lo, the deer, the deer
Comes from her covert of the night! Day
  is here! Day is here, is here!
Lo, the deer! Lo, the deer, the deer!
All creatures wake and see the light. Day
  is here! Day is here, is here!
Day is here! Day is here, is here!

ELEVENTH RITUAL

CHANT TO THE SUN

On this, the second day of the ceremony,
we remember our father the Sun. The sun
comes directly from Tiráwa atius, and who-
ever is touched by the first rays of the sun
in the morning receives new life and

strength which have been brought straight
from the power above. The first rays of
the sun are like a young man, they have not
yet spent their force or grown old, so, to
be touched by them is to receive an acces-
sion of strength.

All the time I am singing this song I
remember the Sun, the Moon, the Stars, the
Corn; all these were made by Tiráwa atius,
and I ask them to give us success and
plenty; success in hunting and in war;
plenty of food, of children, and of health.
The Sun, the Moon, the Stars, the Corn,
are powerful.

We speak of the sun as Father breathing
forth life (h'Aars), causing the earth to
bring forth, making all things to grow. We
think of the sun, which comes direct from
Tiráwa atius, the father of life, and his ray
(hukawi) as the bearer of this life. (You
have seen this ray as it comes through a
little hole or crack.) While we sing, this
ray enters the door of the lodge to bring
strength and power to all within.

The first four verses of this chant are
sung in the morning; they follow the move-
ments of the ray. When the spot has
reached the floor we stop singing and do
not begin again until the afternoon, so that
our song can accompany the ray as it leaves

the lodge, touches the hills, and finally returns to the sun.

I

Now behold; hither comes the ray of our
    father Sun; it cometh over all the land,
    passeth in the lodge, us to touch, and
    give us strength.

II

Now behold, where alights the ray of our
    father Sun; it touches lightly on the
    rim the place above the fire, whence the
    smoke ascends on high.

III

Now behold; softly creeps the ray of our
    father Sun; now o'er the rim it creeps
    to us, climbs down within the lodge;
    climbing down, it comes to us.

IV

Now behold; nearer comes the ray of our
    father Sun; it reaches now the floor
    and moves within the open space, walk-
    ing there, the lodge about.

Later, when the sun is sinking in the
west, the land is in shadow, only on the top
of the hills toward the east can the spot,
the sign of the ray's touch, be seen.   Then

we sing the stanza as we go around the lodge the third time.

The ray of Father Sun, who breathes forth life, is standing on the edge of the hills. We remember that in the morning it had stood on the edge of the opening in the roof of the lodge over the fireplace; now it stands on the edge of the hills that, like the walls of a lodge, inclose the land where the people dwell.

V

Now behold where has passed the ray of
    our father Sun; around the lodge the
    ray has passed and left its blessing
    there, touching us, each one of us.

VI

Now behold; softly climbs the ray of our
    father Sun; it upward climbs, and o'er
    the rim it passes from the place whence
    the smoke ascends on high.

VII

Now behold on the hills the ray of our
    father Sun; it lingers there as loath to
    go, while all the plain is dark. Now
    has gone the ray from us.

VIII

Now behold; lost to us the ray of our father
    Sun; beyond our sight the ray has
    gone, returning to the place whence it
    came to bring us strength.

CHANT OF THE EAGLES

This song likens the bustle and stir of the
Hako party as it comes into the village to
the flapping of the wings of a flock of birds
as they come to a place and alight. It re-
fers also to the birds represented on the
feathered stems—the eagle, the duck, the
woodpecker, and the owl. The noise of the
wings of these birds is what is meant, for
they are moving with the Fathers toward
the Children.

The Wings of the Mighty

I

Hark, the sound of their wings! Mighty
　　birds are here now alighting, bearing
　　promised good.
Hark, the sound of their wings! Surely the
　　Hako is coming.   Children, forward
　　bring your gifts.

II

Hark, the sound of their wings! Mighty
　　birds are here now alighting, bearing
　　promised good.
Hark, the sound of their wings! See! The
　　Hako has come. We children forward
　　bring our gifts.

TWELFTH RITUAL (Second Night)

THE RITES CAME BY A VISION

First Song

Was it, we ask, in dreams that the Fathers
    saw
Clearly the Hako, wherewith I make you
    now
As my son,
My own begotten?
Was it in dreams they learned how to make
    you thus
 My offspring?

Truly, in dreams it was that the Fathers
    saw
Clearly the Hako, wherewith I make you
    now
As my son,
My own begotten.
Truly, in dreams they learned how to make
    you thus
My offspring.

Second Song

This is the teaching, this is the word sent
Down to us from our fathers:

All of the wise words, all of the good gifts,
Brought unto you as a Son,
Verily, through a dream all of these things,
All, by the east descended.

This is the teaching, this is the word sent
Down to us from our fathers:
All of the wise words, all of the good gifts,
Now brought to you as my Son,
Verily, as of old, all of these things,
All, by the east descended.

Third Song—To the Pleiades

Look as they rise, up rise
Over the line where sky meets the earth;
Pleiades!
Lo! They ascending, come to guide us,
Leading us safely, keeping us one;
Pleiades,
Us teach to be, like you, united.

Fourth Song—Of Katasha, the Dwelling Place of the Visions

I

Give heed. We tell of Katasha holy,
Whence the dreams come down, when draw-
    eth the night time near;

Near the gods is their dwelling,
They who watch o'er men; all silently come
    they down.

II

Give heed! The bird of whom we are tell-
    ing
Sends the dreams to us, when draweth the
    night time near;
Kawas, she that is sending
Holy visions, bringing, silently bringing
    peace.

III

Give heed!   The birds of whom we are tell-
    ing
Climb with dreams to us, when draweth the
    night time near;
Down the path they are climbing;
Where the gods to men are traveling come
    they down.

IV

They climb, these birds; a dream each is
    bringing;
Bear they dreams to us, when draweth the
    night time near;
Kawas—she that is sending
Down the birds with dreams; so faithful
    the Hako birds!

V

Then back they speed, the birds that were
bringing
Down the dreams that come when draweth
the night time near;
Birds and dreams are ascending
Where the gods are dwelling, watching
there over men.

VI

Now this we know in truth—where are rest-
ing
Dreams that come to us when draweth the
night time near;
True it is that he did see them;
In a vision saw he Katasha, where they
dwell.

Fifth Song

I

Mother Corn! Mother Corn! We pray
thee,
Be our leader, foes entrapping!
Trusting in thee, we wander far, yet we see
no foe;
Food is gone, hope is dead within us.

II

Then in dreams Mother Corn spoke to me:
"I will lead you, foes entrapping!
"Testing your courage, far have I let you
     go astray;
"Rise, my child, follow me to vict'ry!"

Sixth Song

I

As I lay sleeping, as I lay dreaming,
Out of the distance came one advancing
One whom I ne'er had seen before, but
     when her voice addressed me, straight-
     way I knew her—
Lo! 'Twas our Mother, she whom we
     know.

II

I rose from sleeping, my dream remem-
     b'ring
Her words I pondered, words of our
     mother,
Then I asked of each one I met, Tell me,
     how far may her shrine be? When I
     found it
Sweet smoke I offered unto our Mother.

THE SACRED FEAST OF THE CORN TAKES PLACE

PART II

First Song—To Our Father Sun

> Father, unto thee we cry;
> Father thou of gods and men;
> Father thou of all we hear;
> Father thou of all we see;
> Father, unto thee we cry.

Second Song

Father! Thou above, father of the gods,
They who can come near and touch us,
Do thou bid them bring us help.
Help we need. Father, hear us!

Third Song—To Our Mother Earth

I

Behold! Our Mother Earth is lying here.
Behold! She giveth of her fruitfulness.
Truly, her power gives she us.
Give thanks to Mother Earth who lieth
    here.

II

Behold on Mother Earth the growing fields!
Behold the promise of her fruitfulness!
Truly, her power gives she us.
Give thanks to Mother Earth who lieth
here.

III

Behold on Mother Earth the spreading
trees!
Behold the promise of her fruitfulness!
Truly, her power gives she us.
Give thanks to Mother Earth who lieth
here.

IV

We see on Mother Earth the running
streams;
We see the promise of her fruitfulness.
Truly, her power gives she us.
Our thanks to Mother Earth who lieth
here!

FOURTEENTH RITUAL (Third Night)

INVOKING THE VISIONS OF THE ANCIENTS

I

Oh, come hither,
Holy dreams—Our fathers knew them—
Hither come to us!

Thanks we give unto them.   They our mes-
    sage will hear,
Calling them to come.

II

This way come they,
Holy dreams—Our fathers knew them—
Come they now this way.
Thanks we give unto them.   Coming now,
    they draw near,
Coming now this way.

III

They come nearer,
Holy dreams—Our fathers knew them—
Come they now this way.
Thanks we give unto them.   On the thresh-
    old stand they,
Holy visions stand.

IV

Now then enter,
Holy dreams—Our fathers knew them—
Enter now the lodge.
Thanks we give unto them.   Enter they the
    lodge now,
Enter now the lodge.

V

The Son they see,
Holy dreams—Our fathers knew them—
See him now within.

Thanks we give unto them.   Entered now,
    they see him,
See the Son within.

VI

Now they hover,
Holy dreams—Our fathers knew them—
Hover us above.
Thanks we give unto them.   Pausing here
    above us,
Hover they above.

VII

Now depart they,
Holy dreams—Our fathers knew them—
Now they go away.
Thanks we give unto them.   They are pass-
    ing from us,
Going from the lodge.

VIII

Above rest they,
Holy dreams—Our fathers knew them—
Rest they now above.
Thanks we give unto them.   Where they
    rest we send thanks,
Thanks send far above.

THE FLOCKING OF THE BIRDS

In the early spring the birds lay their
eggs in their nests, in the summer they rear
their young, in the fall all the young ones
are grown, the nests are deserted and the

birds fly in flocks over the country. One
can hear the fluttering of a startled flock,
the birds suddenly rise and their wings
make a noise like distant thunder. Every-
where the flocks are flying. In the fall it
seems as though new life were put into the
people as well as into the birds; there is
much activity in coming and going.

When the eggs are hatched and the young
are grown, the birds flock; the promise of
young has been fulfilled. In this song,
which we sing toward the close of the cere-
mony, we are thinking of the fulfilling of
the promise given by the Hako, that chil-
dren will be granted to the people, so that
they may be many and strong, and we sing
that the great flocks are coming.

I

All around the birds in flocks are flying;
Dipping, rising, circling, see them coming.
See, many birds are flocking here,
All about us now together coming.

II

Yonder see the birds in flocks come flying;
Dipping, rising, circling, see them gather.
Loud is the sound their winging makes,
Rushing come they on the trees alighting!

III

From the flock an eagle now comes flying;
Dipping, rising, circling, comes she hither.

Loud screams the eagle, flying swift.
As an eagle flies, her nestlings seeking.
IV
It is Kawas coming, Kawas flying;
Dipping, rising, circling, she advances.
See! Nearer comes she, nearer comes.
Now, alighted, she her nest is making.
V
Yonder people like the birds are flocking,
See them circling, this side, that side com-
    ing.
Loud is the sound their moving makes,
As together come they, onward come they.
VI
Toward the lodge where sits the Son they
    hasten,
Bringing forward gifts with joyful shout-
    ing.
Hark! Now they like the eagle scream,
Glad of heart, as when her nest she seeth.

FIFTEENTH RITUAL

SONGS FOR THE SIXTEEN CIRCUITS OF THE LODGE

The life of man depends upon the earth
(h'Atira). Tiráwa atius works through it.
The kernel is planted within Mother Earth

and she brings forth the ear of corn, even
as children are begotten and born of
women.

First Song

I

Look on her! She who sought far and near
    for a Son!
Look on her! She who led from afar unto
    you!

II

Thanks we give unto her who came here
    for a Son.
Thanks we give unto her who has led us to
    you.
Thanks we give, Mother Corn, breathing
    life on us all.

Second Song

I

Rev'rent our hearts turn unto the one who
    brings to us
Long life and children, peace, and the gifts
    of strength and food.
Rev'rent our hearts turn unto our Mother
    Corn!

II

Rev'rent our hearts turn unto the source
    whence come to us

Long life and children, peace, and the gifts
of strength and food,
Gifts from Tiráwa, sent through our
Mother Corn.

Third Song
I
O'er the prairie flits in ever widening circ-
les the shadow of a bird about me as I
walk;
Upward turn my eyes, Kawas looks upon
me, she turns with flapping wings and
far away she flies.
II
Round about a tree in ever widening circles
an eagle flies, alertly watching o'er his
nest;
Loudly whistles he, a challenge sending
far, o'er the country wide it echoes
there defying foes.

Fourth Song
I
Kawas flying where her nestlings now are
crying; loudly cry they when they hear
her wings;
Kawas flying, cry her children, as they hear
her come.
'Tis Kawas who now homeward comes!
'Tis Kawas who now homeward comes!

Quickly flying as she hears her young ones
in the nest.

II

Kawas flying, o'er us flying, we her nest-
lings cry for joy as now we see her
come

Kawas flying! Glad our hearts as now we
see her come.

'Tis Kawas brings us good gifts! 'Tis Ka-
was brings us good gifts!

Kawas brings gifts to us; we, like her nest-
lings, cry.

Fifth Song

I

Atira comes, she brings you life, she gives
you joy; to her give thanks as she
draws near.

Now in the lodge before our eyes Atira
moves;

Look upon her who brings you life, who
gives you joy. Oh, offer thanks to
Mother Corn!

II

The Hako comes within the lodge, it walks
within; let us give thanks as it draws
near.

Now in the lodge with Mother Corn the
Hako moves;

Thanks do we give for all the joy it brings
to us, the children here, from realms
above.

Sixth Song

I

I know not if the voice of man can reach to
the sky;
I know not if the mighty one will hear as I
pray;
I know not if the gifts I ask will all granted
be;
I know not if the word of old we truly can
hear;
I know not what will come to pass in our fu-
ture days;
I hope that only good will come, my chil-
dren, to you.

II

I now know that the voice of man can reach
to the sky;
I now know that the mighty one has heard
as I prayed;
I now know that the gifts I asked have all
granted been;
I now know that the word of old we truly
have heard;
I now know that Tiráwa hearkens unto
man's prayer;

I know that only good has come, my children, to you.

SIXTEENTH RITUAL
(Fifth Day, Dawn)

SEEKING THE CHILD

The child referred to is usually a little son or daughter of the Son, the man who has received the Hako party. Upon this little child we are to put the signs of the promises which Mother Corn and Kawas bring, the promise of children, of increase, of long life, of plenty. The signs of these promises are put upon this little child, but they are not merely for that particular child but for its generation, that the children already born may live, grow in strength, and in their turn increase so that the family and the tribe may continue.

First Song

With the dawn will I seek, seek my child,
Among the Children seek
One the gods shall here make;
My offspring, my own child.

Second Song

I

Where is he, the Son?
Where his dwelling place that I seek?
Which can be his lodge, where he sits
Silent, waiting, waiting there for me?

II

Here is he, the Son,
Here his dwelling place that I seek;
This here is his lodge where he sits
Silent, waiting, waiting here for me.

SYMBOLIC INCEPTION

First Song

The ear of corn represents h'Uraru,
Mother Earth who brings forth; the power
which causes her to bring forth is from
above, and the blue paint represents that
power.

We hold the painted ear of corn toward
the little child that the powers from above
and from below may come near it.

Now our eyes look on him who is here;
He is as the Son we have sought;
He brings us again tidings of the Son:
"Father, come to me, here I sit
Waiting here for thee."

SIXTEENTH RITUAL

PART II

Second Song

While we sing the third stanza, the Ku-
rahus touches the little child on the fore-
head with the ear of corn. The spirit of
Mother Corn, with the power of Mother
Earth, granted from above, has touched
the child.

The touch means the promise of fruitful-
ness to the child and its generation.

I

Tirawa, harken! Mighty one
Above us in blue, silent sky!
We standing wait thy bidding here;
The Mother Corn standing waits,
Waits to serve thee here;
The Mother Corn stands waiting here.

II

Tirawa, harken! Mighty one
Above us in blue, silent sky!
We touch upon thy country fair;
The Mother Corn touches there
Upon the border land;
The Mother Corn is touching there.

III

Tirawa, harken! Mighty one
Above us in blue, silent sky!
The path we reach leads up to thee;
The Mother Corn enters there,
Upward takes her way;
The Mother Corn to thee ascends.

IV

Tirawa, harken! Mighty one
Above us in blue, silent sky!
Behold! We in thy dwelling stand;
The Mother Corn, standing there,
Leader now is made;
The Mother Corn is leader made.

Third Song

This song means that it is accomplished, that the child has been encompassed by the powers represented by the united stems. It is a promise of procreation.

I

Here stand we while upon Tirawa now we
    wait;
Here Kawas stands, her mate with her is
    standing here;
They both are standing, waiting, bringing
    gifts with them.

II

We finished are, as on Tirawa now we wait;
The task of Kawas with her mate accomplished is,
And all the work they came to do is finished now.

ACTION SYMBOLIZING LIFE

The child, surrounded by the creative forces, is urged to move, to arise as the first song is sung.

The four steps taken by the child represent the progress of life.

First Song

I am ready; come to me now, fearing nothing; come now to me here.
Little one, come, come to me here; fearing nothing, come.

Second Song

Stepping forward is my child, he forward steps, the four steps takes and enters into life;
Forward stepping, four steps taking, enters into life.

Third Song

Here we go singing, looking on the child
Borne in his father's arms, he leading us;
Follow me singing, looking on the child.

SEVENTEENTH RITUAL

TOUCHING THE CHILD

On the preceding night water was taken
from a stream; this water is now put into
a bowl. Every detail of this act is sym-
bolic. The time when the water was ob-
tained was night, the mother of day; run-
ning water symbolizes the continuity of
life, one generation following another; the
bowl which holds the water resembles in
its shape the dome of the sky, the abode of
the powers which bestow life.

The child is touched with the water upon
the head and face, an invisible outline be-
ing made, which afterward is to become
distinct. The first touching with water,
one of the lesser powers, is to cleanse and
give strength.

First Song

I

Give heed, my child, lift your eyes, behold
the one who is standing here;

Behold, my child; waiting here to bring
    the gift of strength to you.
Give heed, my child. Look! Water waits
    to bring to you gift of strength.

II

Give heed, my child, lift your eyes, behold
    the one who has brought you strength
Behold, my child! Strength you have and
    finished is the task.
Give heed, my child. Look! Water now
    has brought to you gift of strength.

Water is for sustenance and the main-
tenance of health; it is one of the great
gifts of Tirawa atius.

The white man speaks of a heavenly
Father; we say Tirawa atius, the Father
above, but we do not think of Tirawa as a
person. We think of Tirawa as in every-
thing, as the power which has arranged
and thrown down from above everything
the man needs. What the power above,
Tirawa atius, is like, no one knows, no one
has been there.

ANOINTING THE CHILD

As we sing this song the old man makes
the same lines upon the face of the child

as he made with the water and the brush
of grass. This is in recognition that the
life which has been sustained and nour-
ished is now consecrated to Tirawa atius,
the father above, who gives life to all
things.

I

Give heed, my child, lift your eyes, behold
    the one who is standing here,
Behold, my child! waiting now to fit and
    set you here apart.
Give heed, my child. Look! Sacred oint-
    ment now is here come to you.

II

Give heed, my child, lift your eyes, behold
    the one who has holy made.
Behold, my child! You are set apart, and
    finished is the task.
Give heed, my child. Look! Sacred oint-
    ment now has set you apart.

Second Song

The grass of which the brush is made is
gathered during a ceremony belonging to
the Rain shrine. It represents Toharu, the
living covering of Mother Earth. The
power which is in Toharu gives food to
man and the animals so that they can live
and become strong and able to perform

the duties of life. This power represented
by the brush of grass is now standing be-
fore the little child.

While we sing this song the old man
touches the forehead of the child with the
brush of grass. The power of Toharu has
reached the child, has come in contact with
it to impart the strength that comes from
food.

I

Give heed, my child, lift your eyes, behold
 the one who is standing here;
Behold, my child! waiting here to bring
 the gift of food to you.
Give heed, my child. Look! Grass now
 waits to bring to you gift of food.

II

Give heed, my child, lift your eyes, behold
 the one who has brought you food.
Behold, my child! Food you have received,
 and finished is the task.
Give heed, my child. Look! Grass has
 now here brought you the gift of food.

PAINTING THE CHILD

First Song

The paint symbolizes the red clouds of
the dawn, the coming of the new day, the
rising sun, the vigor of life. The power

of the new day, the new life, is now stand-
ing before the child.

As we sing this song the old man touches
the forehead with the red paint. The
vigor of life, the power of the touch of the
sun, is now on the child.

I

Give heed, my child, lift your eyes, behold
the one who is standing here,
Behold, my child! waiting to bring the gift
of life to you.
Give heed, my child. Look! Red paint
waits, the vigor of life to bring.

II

Give heed, my child, lift your eyes, behold
the one who has brought you life.
Behold, my child. Life you have received
and finished is the task.
Give heed, my child. Look. Red paint
leaves the vigor of life with you.

Second Song

Blue represents the sky, the place where
Tirawa atius dwells, and with this blue
paint we are to make upon the child a pic-
ture of the face of Tirawa atius. It is a
mark of Tirawa atius' acceptance of the
consecrated child and a sign of his pres-
ence. The symbol of the dwelling place of
Tirawa atius stands before the child.

I

Give heed, my child, lift your eyes, behold
    the one who is standing here,
Behold, my child! waiting here to make the
    sign of him above.
Give heed, my child. Look! Blue paint
    waits to bring to you sign of him.

II

Give heed, my child, lift your eyes, behold
    the one who has brought the sign,
Behold, my child! brought to you the sign.
    Accomplished now the task.
Give heed, my child. Look! Blue paint
    now has left with you sign of him.

PUTTING ON THE SYMBOLS

First Song

The down represents the high, light
clouds (cirrus) in the blue of the sky; they
are near the abode of Tirawa atius.

The down is taken from under the wings
of the white eagle. The white eagle is the
mate of the brown eagle, and the child is
the child of Kawas, the brown eagle. The
down grew close to the heart of the eagle
and moved as the eagle breathed. It rep-
resents the breath and life of the white
eagle, the father of the child.

While we sing this song the old man
opens his hand and lets the down fall upon
the hair. The soft, white clouds near the
abode of Tirawa atius have dropped and
covered the head of the child.

I

Give heed, my child, lift your eyes, behold
  the one who is standing here,
Behold, my child! waiting here to bring
  the sign of clouds above.
Give heed, my child. Look! Down of eagle
  waits with the sign of clouds.

II

Give heed, my child, lift your eyes, behold
  the one who has laid on you,
Behold, my child! sign of fleecy clouds that
  near Tirawa float.
Give heed, my child. Look! Rests on you
  sign of the clouds above.

We sing in the fifth stanza that it is ac-
complished, the head of the consecrated
child now rests in the soft, white clouds
which float near the dwelling place of
Tirawa atius.

Second Song

While we sing this song, the old man ties
the downy feather on the child's hair.

Tirawa atius is now with the little child as
the double feather waves over its head.

I

Give heed, my child, lift your eyes, behold
    the one who is standing here,
Behold, my child! waiting here to bring
    the last great gift to you.
Give heed, my child. Look! Waits to
    bring the emblem the Father sends.

II

Give heed, my child, lift your eyes, behold
    the one who has left on you,
Behold, my child! left on you Tirawa's
    breathing sign.
Give heed, my child. Look! On you rests
    the emblem the Father sent.

Now we sing that all is accomplished.
The child has been fully prepared, the
sacred symbols put upon it, the powers
from above have come, and Tirawa atius
breathes over it.

The child is now told to look into the
bowl of water and behold its face. The
running water symbolizes the passing on of
generations, one following another. The
little child looks on the water and sees its
own likeness, as it will see that likeness in
its children and children's children. The
face of Tirawa atius is there also, giving

promise that the life of the child shall go on, as the waters flow over the land.

EIGHTEENTH RITUAL

FULFILMENT PREFIGURED

Making the Nest

The circle represents a nest, and is drawn by the toe because the eagle builds its nest with its claws. Although we are imitating the bird making its nest, there is another meaning to the action; we are thinking of Tirawa making the world for the people to live in. If you go on a high hill and look around, you will see the sky touching the earth on every side, and within this circular inclosure the people live. So the circles we have made are not only nests, but they also represent the circle Tirawa atius has made for the dwelling place of all the people. The circles also stand for the kinship group, the clan, and the tribe.

The down represents the light clouds near the dwelling place of Tirawa—the dome of the sky over the dwelling place of the people—and it stands for the protection of Tirawa.

Song

Behold where two eagles come forth!
Now they soar high over head:
See where one flies, watching, flies, guard-
      ing he
His mate who has gone to her nest, drop-
      ping there;
'Tis Kawas who brings there new life.

SYMBOLIC FULFILMENT

The child represents the young genera-
tion, the continuation of life, and when it is
put in the circle it typifies the bird laying
its eggs.

Song

Within the nest the child rests its little
      feet,
Awaiting there the gift sent by gods above;
Descending there to him comes the prom-
      ised life.

THANK OFFERING

An offering of sweet smoke is made to
Tirawa; then all traces of the nest are ob-
literated, and the lodge is once more
thrown open to the people.

NINETEENTH RITUAL

THE CALL TO THE CHILDREN

The purpose of the rite is recognized by the important place given to children in this part of the ceremony. The ponies presented to the Fathers are each led up by a little child; the acting out of a man's war-like deeds is to honor his child, and the little child with the black covering upon its head and the picture of Tirawa upon its face receives, with the chief, the gifts as they are presented.

In every instance the child is the tie between the two groups, the Fathers and Children.

First Song

Harken! List! We are calling you. Come!
    Come! Children, come!
Come! We're ready and waiting, your
    Father's waiting. Come! Children,
    come!
Hear us calling, calling you! Children,
    come!
Children, come! Come hither!
Harken! List as we call you, call to the
    Children to come.

Second Song

Ready and waiting, we call you, loud we
    call you, loudly call;
"Come to us, Children," call we loudly,
    call we long; Oh, come!
Come! Come! Come!
Hear us calling, calling, Children! Oh,
    come!
Hear us calling, come to us here! Come!

Third Song

Look, where they come, see them, see them,
    young ones and old ones!
Look! Here they come, this way, that way
    flocking together.
Hither they come, shouting like eagles,
Shouting come.
Joyous, happy, gladly come they, gaily
    coming, coming hither.
See where they come, flocking like birds,
    shouting like eagles
As they come to the Fathers.

TWENTIETH RITUAL

BLESSING THE CHILD

When I sing this song I pray to Tirawa
to come down and touch with his breath the
symbol of his face and all the other sym-

bols on the little child. I pray with all my spirit that Tirawa atius will let the child grow up and become strong and find favor in its life.

This is a very solemn act, because we believe that Tirawa atius, although not seen by us, sends down his breath as we pray, calling on him to come.

As I sing this song here with you I can not help shedding tears. I have never sung it before except as I stood looking upon the little child and praying for it in my heart. There is no little child here, but you are here writing all these things down that they may not be lost and that our children may know what their fathers believed and practiced in this ceremony. So, as I sing, I am calling to Tirawa atius to send down his breath upon you, to give you strength and long life. I am praying for you with all my spirit.

The purport of this song is hidden from the people, but this is what it means: All that I have been doing to you, little child, has been a prayer to call down the breath of Tirawa atius to give you long life and strength and to teach you that you belong to him—that you are his child and not mine.

Song

Breathe on him!
Breathe on him!
Life thou alone canst give to him.
Long life, we pray, Oh Father, give unto
    him!

INCIDENTAL RITUALS

I

COMFORTING THE CHILD

Long ago there lived a holy man who
knew all the songs and the rites of this
ceremony, and to him came a vision where-
in he was taught how to bring comfort to
a little child when, during the ceremony, it
cried and could not be pacified. In this
vision he was shown what he must do to
bring comfort to the little child, and he
heard the songs that he must sing. The
songs which he heard have been handed
down through many generations.

When during the ceremony a child cries
and can not be comforted, the mother, or
some one sent by her, can approach the Ku-
rahus who carries the brown-eagle stem
and ask him to comfort and quiet the child.

The Kurahus must comply with this request, so he rises and stands before the holy place, takes up the feathered stem and sings this song, which tells the brown eagle, Kawas, that its baby is crying.

First Song

Kawas, harken; thy baby is crying!
It grieveth, wailing and weeping and crying so sore.
Ah! It cries, cryeth so sorely;
Kawas, hasten, thy little one cryeth so sore.

Second Song

Father cometh, now he cometh;
See him, little one; hark! his footsteps!
With him, see! coming are the eagles,
All are coming now to thee.

Third Song

I

Look, my child, who is coming unto you;
Look up, my little one, now your trouble goes away, away;
Look! Above you flies one who guards you,

Whose presence brings you joy. Now your
    sorrow has departed.

II

Ah, you look! See the eagles flying over
    you.
From up above they come, from the clear
    blue sky where Father dwells;
They to you this peace-bringing solace
    give.
A happy little child now is smiling here
    light-hearted.

II

CHANGING A MAN'S NAME

If any man of the Son's party had
achieved success in war, and his achieve-
ments had been acknowledged by the peo-
ple, he could request the Son to have the
ceremony of changing his name performed.

This dramatic poem is in a rhythmic
form impossible to reproduce in English;
neither is a literal translation adequate to
convey its meaning, since a single word
sometimes represents a complex action, to
the understanding of which a knowledge of
the customs and beliefs of the tribe is essen-
tial. The terseness of expression was also
intended to close the meaning to the un-
initiated, keeping it sacred from the com-

mon people. Although the form of the following rhythmic rendition could not be determined as heretofore by musical phrases, the English version contains nothing which is not in the original text explained and amplified by the Kurahus.

The ritual is in three parts. The first gives a brief narration of the institution of the custom of changing the name in consequence of some new achievement. The second shows how the man was enabled to accomplish this act. It began with his lonely vigil and fast, when he cried to the powers for help. The scene then shifts to the circle of the lesser powers, who, in council, deliberate on the petition which makes its way to them and gains their consent. Then the Winds summon the messengers, and these, gathering at the lesser powers' command, are sent to earth to the man crying in lonely places, to grant his desire. This part closes with a few vivid words which set forth that only by the favor and help of the powers had the man been able to do the deed. The third deals with the man's names, the one to be discarded and the one now to be assumed.

Harken! 'Twas thus it came to pass:
In ancient days, a Leader and his men

Walked this wide earth, man's vast
 abode
Roofed by the heavens, where dwell the
 gods.
They reached a place, the spot no man
 can tell,
Faced dangers dread, and vanquished
 them:
Then, standing as if born anew to life
Each warrior threw away the name
That had been his ere yet these deeds
 were done.

Harken! The Leader and his men
 Made there the Vict'ry Song, and set the
  mark!
 Ye must o'ertake, if ye would be like
  them!

Harken! The Leader and his men
 Turned then toward home. Their Vict'ry
  Song
 Proclaimed them near; the village rose,
 Looked toward the hill, where on the top
 Stood the brave men singing their Song,
 Heralding thus the favor of the gods
 By which they had surpassed all former
  deeds,
 Made new their claim to be accounted
  men.

Harken! And whence, think ye, was borne
  Unto these men courage to dare,
  Strength to endure hardship and war?
  Mark well my words, as I reveal
  How the gods help man's feebleness.
  The Leader of these warriors was a man
  Given to prayer. Oft he went forth
  Seeking a place no one could find,
  There would he stand, and lift his voice
  Fraught with desire, that he might be
  Invincible, a bulwark 'gainst all foes
  Threat'ning his tribe, causing them fear.
  Nighttime and day this cry sped on,
  Traveling far, seeking to reach—
Harken! Those places far above—
Harken! Within the circle vast
  Where sit the gods, watching o'er men.

Harken! This poor man's prayer went on,
  Speeding afar into the blue
  Heavens above, reached there the place—
Harken! Where dwell the lesser gods—
Harken! And great Tirawa, mightier than
  all!

Harken! It was because a god
  Received this prayer, considered it,
  Favored its plea, and passed it on
  To him whose place was next, in that
  grand ring,

Who, in his turn received the prayer,
Considered it, and sent it on—
Harken!   Around that circle vast—
Harken!   Where sit the gods above.

Harken!   And thus it was the prayer
Sent by this man won the consent
Of all the gods.   For each god in his
place
Speaks out his thought, grants or rejects
Man's suppliant cry, asking for help;
But none can act until the Council grand
Comes to accord, thinks as one mind,
Has but one will, all must obey.
Harken!   The Council gave consent—
Harken!   And great Tirawa, mightier
than all.

Harken!   To make their purpose known,
Succor and aid freely to give,
Heralds were called, called by the Winds;
Then in the west uprose the Clouds
Heavy and black, ladened with storm.
Slowly they climbed, dark'ning the skies;
While close on every side the Thunders
marched
On their dread way, 'till all were come
To where the gods in stately Council sat
Waiting for them.   Then, bade them go
Back to the earth, carrying aid

To him whose prayers had reached their
circle vast.
This mandate given, the Thunders turned
toward earth,
Taking their course slantwise the sky.

Harken! Another followed hard—
Lightning broke forth out of the Cloud,
Zig-zag and dart, cleaving their way
Slantwise to earth, their goal to reach.

Harken! For these two were not all
That hastened to proclaim the gods' be-
hest;
Swift on their wings, ranging the path,
Black breasts and red, yellow, and
white,
Flying about, clearing the way
For those who bore the message of the
gods
Granting the man courage to dare,
Strength to endure, power to stand
Invincible, a bulwark 'gainst all foes.

Harken! 'Twas thus it came to pass:
The Leader grasped the help sent by the
gods;
Henceforth he walked steadfast and
strong,

Leading his men through dangers drear,
Knowing that naught could strike at him
To whom the gods had promised victory.

Attend!   Once more I change his name!

Harken!   Rirutskatit, it was
We used to call him by, a name he won
Long days ago, marking an act
Well done by him, but now passed by.

Harken!   Today all men shall say—

Harken!   His act has lifted him
Where all his tribe behold a man
Clothed with new fame, strong in new
    strength,
Gained by his deeds, blessed by the gods.
Harken!   Shakúru Wárukote shall he be
    called.

CONCLUSION

LAST WORDS OF TAHIRUSSAWICHI

I have done what has never been done
before. I have given you all the songs of
this ceremony and explained them to you.
I never thought that I, of all my people,

should be the one to give this ancient ceremony to be preserved, and I wonder over it as I sit here.

I think over my long life with its many experiences; of the great number of Pawnees who have been with me in war, nearly all of whom have been killed in battle. I have been severely wounded many times—see this scar over my eye. I was with those who went to the Rocky Mountains to the Cheyennes, when so many soldiers were slain that their dead bodies lying there looked like a great blue blanket spread over the ground. When I think of all the people of my own tribe who have died during my lifetime and then of those in other tribes that have fallen by our hands, they are so many they make a vast cover over Mother Earth. I once walked with these prostrate forms. I did not fall but I passed on, wounded sometimes but not to death, until I am here to-day doing this thing, singing these sacred songs and telling you of these ancient rites of my people. It must be that I have been preserved for this purpose, otherwise I should be lying back there among the dead.

SONGS FROM NORTH AND SOUTH

SONGS FROM NORTH AND SOUTH

These songs, translated by Frances Densmore, together with their music, are to be found in the following bulletins of the Bureau of American Ethnology, Smithsonian Institution: Mandan and Hidatsa, Bulletin 80; Teton Sioux, Bulletin 61; Northern Ute, Bulletin 75; Pawnee, Bulletin 93; Papago, Bulletin 90; Yuman and Yaqui, Bulletin 110. The Tule song, by the same author, is from the Smithsonian publication, ''Music of the Tule Indians.''

MANDAN AND HIDATSA

SONG TO THE RAVEN

Raven
I am going to die—
fly away.

EARTH ALWAYS ENDURES

Earth
always
endures.

HE STARED AT ME

My dear friend
your husband,
at me
how he stared.
Will you throw him away?

YOU DID IT

You did it
therefore
you wept.

343

I CANNOT SLEEP
O
 to sleep
 to lie!
I think, if—
 but I cannot sleep.

SERENADE
 O
  to be a man!

SHE WALKS ALONE
 A certain maiden
  to the garden
  goes;
  lonely
  she walks.

WE MADE FIRE
Comrade,
 in the daytime when we made fire
 it was pleasant.
I understand women.

TETON SIOUX

SONG FOR FAIR WEATHER
 May the sun rise well;
  may the earth appear
  brightly shone upon!

    May the moon rise well;
        may the earth appear
        brightly shone upon!

SONG OF THE SACRED POLE
Father—
    all these he has made me own—
    the trees and the forests
    standing
    in their places.

NOON SONG
Where
    holy
    you behold,
    in the place where the sun rises
    holy
    may you behold.
Where
    holy
    you behold,
    in the place where the sun passes us in
        his course
    holy
    you behold.
Where
    goodness
    you behold,
    at the turning back of the sun
    goodness
    may you behold.

IN A SACRED MANNER I RETURN

Friends
  behold me,
  in a sacred manner
  I return.
You, tribe,
  behold me,
  in a sacred manner
  I return.
The nation sitting holy,
  friends,
  behold me,
  in a sacred manner
  I return.
You, tribe,
  behold me,
  in a sacred manner
  I return.

SONG OF CROW AND OWL

At midnight
  may I roam
  against the winds.
May I roam
  at night.
May I roam
  when the owl
  is hooting—
  may I roam.

At dawn
   may I roam
   against the winds.
May I roam
   at dawn.
May I roam
   when the crow
   is calling—
   may I roam.

WHERE THE WIND IS BLOWING

Where
   the wind
   is blowing,
   the wind is roaring.
   I stand
   westward.
The wind
   is blowing,
   the wind
   is roaring—
   I stand.

EVEN THE EAGLE DIES

Soldiers,
   you fled.
Even the eagle dies.

A WOLF I CONSIDERED MYSELF

A wolf
    I considered myself
    but
    I have eaten nothing,
    therefore
    from standing
    I am tired out.

A wolf
    I considered myself
    but
    the owls are hooting
    and
    the night I fear.

OWLS HOOT AT ME

Owls
    hoot at me;
    owls
    hoot at me.
That is what
    I hear in my life.

Wolves
    howl at me;
    wolves
    howl at me.
That is what
    I hear in my life.

I LOOK FOR HIM IN VAIN

As the young men go by
  I am looking for him.
It surprises me anew
  that he has gone.
It is something
  to which I can not be reconciled.

YOU SHOULD GIVE UP THE WARPATH

  Going on the warpath
    you should give up,
    and you should desire
    to settle down
    and stop for good.

A PRAIRIE FIRE

A prairie fire
  I started
  when you were intent on women
  and hindered by them.
Did you see it?
  well,
  it was I
  who did it.

SONG OF SITTING BULL
A warrior
I have been;
now
it is all over.
A hard time
I have.

SONG OF THE FAMINE
The old men
now are so few
that they are not worth counting.
I myself am
the last living,
therefore
a hard time
I am having.

NORTHERN UTE

DANCE SONG
On a mountain
the noise of the wind.

PAWNEE

UNREAL THE BUFFALO IS
STANDING
He said, unreal the buffalo is standing.
These are his sayings,
unreal the buffalo is standing,
unreal he stands in the open space,
unreal he is standing.

I AM LIKE A BEAR

I am like a bear.
I hold up my hands
   waiting for the sun to rise.

SPRING IS OPENING

Spring is opening.
I can smell the different perfumes
   of the white weeds used in the dance.

THE WHITE FOX

Yonder it comes.
The expanse of earth is wide.
My brother the fox spoke and said,
   "Behold and see the wideness of the
     earth,
   the white foxes know the earth is wide."

IT IS MINE, THIS COUNTRY WIDE

Yonder they are coming.
Although strange misfortunes have befallen
   me,
   yet it is mine, this country wide.

THE THUNDER SPOKE QUIETLY

   Beloved, it is good,
     he is saying quietly,
     the thunder, it is good.

OUR HEARTS ARE SET IN THE HEAVENS
It is there that our hearts are set,
in the expanse of the heavens.

THE HEAVENS ARE SPEAKING
I stood here, I stood there,
the clouds are speaking.
I say, "You are the ruling power,
I do not understand, I only know what I
am told.
You are the ruling power, you are now
speaking.
This power is yours, O heavens."

MAD CHIEF MOURNS FOR HIS GRANDSON
Mad chief sings as he walks,
his spirit is glad as he walks.
Push-Forward is no longer among us,
yet we seem to see him.
Yonder he comes.

PAPAGO

WHITE FEATHERS ALONG THE EDGE OF THE WORLD
Downy white feathers
are moving beneath the sunset
and along the edge of the world.

WHO IS GOING TO MARRY ME
Who are you, nice boys?
Who is going to marry me?

TERRIBLE IN ITS POWER
Hanging motionless in the sky
yet terrible in its power to destroy.

THE MAN WHO HAS NO JOY
Who is the man who killed an enemy
and has no joy?
I am having all the joy alone.

THE WOMAN BY THE SEA SINGS
Where am I running from,
that I come here?
Am I crazy woman
with a painted face?

I MET A MEXICAN
While I was running I met a Mexican who
said,
"How do you do?"
While I was running I met·a Mexican with
a long beard who said,
"How do you do?"

THE BRIGHT MORNING
The bright morning begins to shine.
Get up, three of you, and see Manasi Moun-
tain.

On top of it is yellow water.
I went there, drank the water, and stag-
gered in running.

SINGING TO THE LEAVES AND FLOWERS

Crazy woman, crazy woman, trying to sing
to mescal leaves,
how can she sing to them and make the
wind come?
Young children, trying to sing to *bahwi*
flowers,
how can they sing to *bahwi* flowers and
bring rain?

SONG OF THE HORSE

Black hair rope is what you used in roping
me.
You treated me badly.
You even threw me down and tied me.
Not satisfied with that, you tied a knot in
my tail.
That made me disgusted.

SONG OF THE WHITE MOUNTAIN

A white mountain is far at the west.
It stands beautiful.
It has brilliant white arches of light
bending down toward the earth.

THE LITTLE CAPTIVE CHILDREN

Men shouting "brother,"
   men shouting "brother."
Among the mountains they have
   taken little Apache children
   where the sun went down in sorrow.
All women,
   what shall we do to realize this?

A POOR MAN

A poor man takes the songs in his hand
   and drops them near the place where the
   sun sets.
See, Cowaka, run to them and take them in
   your hand
   and place them under the sunset.

THE WIND BLOWS FROM THE SEA

By the sandy water I breathe in the odor of
   of the sea;
From there the wind comes and blows over
   the world.
By the sandy water I breathe in the odor
   of the sea;
From there the clouds come and rain falls
   over the world.

BEFORE STARTING ON THE WARPATH

I am going to walk far, far,
I hope to have a fine morning somewhere.
I am going to run far, far,
I hope to have a good night somewhere.

THE VOICE OF THE HERALD

When the morning starts and the sun comes
    up,
When the morning starts and the sun comes
    up,
At that time the voice of the herald sounds
    sweet.
It seems to be calling to me.

THE MORNING STAR

The morning star is up.
I cross the mountains
    into the light of the sea.

EVENING SONG

The sun is slowly departing,
It is slower in its setting;
Black bats will be swooping when the sun
    is gone,
  That is all.

The spirit children are beneath,
They are moving back and forth;

They roll in play among tufts of white
    eagle down,
That is all.

IN THE GREAT NIGHT

In the great night my heart will go out;
Toward me the darkness comes rustling.
In the great night my heart will go out.

WE SMOKE TOGETHER
(Sung by an Apache spirit)

It was a sad thing you did;
It was a sad thing you did,
But now we smoke together.
The smoke will gather inside us.

RAIN SONGS
1

Clouds are standing in the east, they are
    approaching,
It rains in the distance;
Now it is raining here and the thunder rolls.

2

Green rock mountains are thundering with
    clouds.
With this thunder the Akim village is shak-
    ing.
The water will come down the arroyo
    and I will float on the water.
Afterward the corn will ripen in the fields.

3

Close to the west the great ocean is singing.
The waves are rolling toward me, covered
with many clouds.
Even here I catch the sound.
The earth is shaking beneath me and I
hear deep rumbling.

4

A cloud on top of Evergreen Mountain is
singing,
A cloud on top of Evergreen Mountain is
standing still.
It is raining and thundering up there,
It is raining here.
Under the mountain the corn tassels are
shaking,
Under the mountain the slender spikes of
child corn are glistening.

YUMAN AND YAQUI

(Colorado River Basin)

*THE WATER BUG AND THE
SHADOWS*

The water bug
is drawing
the shadows of the evening
toward him on the water.

THE DEER IS TAKING AWAY THE DAYLIGHT

The deer is taking away the daylight.
After taking away the daylight
  he named it Darkness.

SONG OF ADMIRATION

In Cocori is a young girl
  whose name is Hesucita.
She is a pretty girl,
  her eyes look like stars;
  her pretty eyes are like stars moving.

THE OWL HOOTED

The owl was requested
  to do as much as he knew how.
He only hooted and told of the morning
    star,
And hooted again and told of the dawn.

THE BUSH IS SINGING

The bush is sitting
under a tree
and singing.

THE RISING SUN

The sun is coming up.
It is time to go out
and see the clouds.

THE DEER AND THE FLOWER

The deer
looks at a flower.

SONG OF BROWN BUZZARD AFTER REMOVING HIS SCALP

You must enjoy yourselves in the evening.
Look at me. See how I look
and yet I am happy.

TULE

(*Panama*)

TULE LOVE SONG

Many pretty flowers, red, blue and yellow;
we say to the girls, "Let us go and walk
among the flowers."
The wind comes and sways the flowers,
the girls are like that when they dance;
some are wide-open, large flowers and
some are tiny little flowers.
The birds love the sunshine and the star-
light;
the flowers smell sweet.
The girls are sweeter than the flowers.